BEING AT LEISURE

PLAYING AT LIFE

About The Author

Dr. Bruno Hans Geba,
Professor, Philosopher,
Psychotherapist

Dr. Geba was born in Salzburg, Austria and received his graduate training in psychology, physical education and the basic medical sciences at the University of Vienna. From 1951 to 1954 he served as an advisor to the Iranian Ministry of Health and Education and held a guest professorship at the University of Tehran. In 1955 he was invited to the United States as a consultant by the Aspen Institute for Humanistic Studies and directed its Health Center until 1962. After four years with the University of New Mexico and the Lovelace Foundation for Medical Research, he obtained his American doctorate at the University of Colorado. The following year he traveled around the world with the University of the Seven Seas. In 1966 he settled in San Francisco where he conducted his private practice and served as a consultant and professor for the California School of Professional Psychology. Since 1975 Dr. Geba has been a professor of Recreation Therapy at San Diego State University. His latest books, *Breathe Away Your Tension, Vitality Training for Older Adults* and *Being at Leisure—Playing at Life* are examples of his unique approach to preventive medicine and the art of living.

BEING AT LEISURE
PLAYING AT LIFE

A GUIDE TO HEALTH
AND JOYFUL LIVING

Bruno Hans Geba

LEISURE
SCIENCE
SYSTEMS INTERNATIONAL

First Printing, March, 1985:   500 copies in cloth
                               5000 copies in paperback

Cover by Bardy Anderson

Figures by Anne Brook

Library of Congress Cataloging in Publication Data:

  Geba, Bruno Hans, 1927–
    Being at leisure, playing at life.

    1. Leisure   2. Recreation
  I. Title.
  GV53.G42 1985   790'.01'350973   84-82403
  ISBN 0-932057-01-2
  ISBN 0-932057-00-4 (pbk.)

Manufactured in the United States of America

To

Dorian and Peter

Table of Contents

PART I
BEING AT LEISURE

PART II
PLAYING AT LIFE

The terms, individuals, people, persons, humanity and humans are applied interchangeably throughout the book. Man or mankind and the respective pronouns are used strictly in the generic sense and embrace individuals of both sexes.

PART I

BEING AT LEISURE

1

Recreation – A Sleeping Giant

Recreation. What does it mean to you? Is it free time, fun, relaxation, relief from work or merely *"Dolce far niente,"* the sweetness of doing nothing, as the Italians say? When you hear or see the word *recreation,* what comes to your mind? Do you think of yourself skiing in two feet of powder snow, sailing into the horizon, climbing a rock face, swimming in the ocean, making love, listening to music, or reading a book? How does it make you feel? Do you get all quiet inside, joyful, excited, or are you totally lost in the moment?

Recreation, I am sure, means different things to different people. But are there any characteristics that are unique to recreation, that give it a very special place in the lifestyle pattern of today's world? I think so. And I'd like to share with you some of my ideas about the uniqueness of recreation.

Today, the word recreation is widely used, and is part of the vocabulary of thousands of people. This hasn't always been the case. Not too long ago, when I first was invited to the United States in 1955 as a consultant to the Aspen Institute for Humanistic Studies, the big recreation boom hadn't started yet. Skiing in this country, for instance, was still in its infancy and almost all of the ski equipment had to be imported from Europe.

Mr. Head was just beginning to experiment with the design and production of his revolutionary metal ski. I used to test ski some of these early models, and I can still remember trying out the very first plastic boots at about the same time. Then too, my own hiking boots and leather backpack were rarities even in a mountain resort like Aspen. These were the days before jogging and bicycling had become pastimes for the general public. It was also a time when concepts of leisure were discussed rather esoterically during the seminars of the Aspen Institute by philosophers and sociologists like Mortimer Adler[1] and Reuel Denney[2]. In academic institutions, recreation as an independent discipline was hardly represented at all. At best, it functioned only as an inferior adjunct to physical education. Half-serious jokes equating recreation with "throwing out the ball" and "lighting campfires" were commonplace.

Times change and so do people. During the past twenty years, recreation has entered the lives of the masses. The growth of the field of recreation has been spectacular. And growth is very desirable indeed, particularly when growing is synonymous with maturing. But unfortunately, as is often the case, an increase in quantity occurs at the expense of quality. Rapid growth then results in conflicting interests, fragmentation and a loss of cohesiveness. This can easily be seen when a community expands too fast; it begins to suffer from such common maladies as over speculation in real estate, poor planning, inadequate resources and political turmoil. People become preoccupied with vested interests and lose touch with the values that used to bring them together. As a result, they end up with the type of urban sprawls that almost instantly self-destruct into hopeless slums.

A similar dilemma has been created by the incredible expansion of recreation during the past 25 years. Particularly in the affluent countries of the modern world, the exploitation of the leisure explosion has been phenomenal. In the late sixties, for instance, when I lived in San Francisco, it was nearly impossible to find a bicycle with a lightweight frame. Now they are lined up in bike shops across the country with the most sophisticated racing and touring gear available. And what is more important, people are buying them by the carload. Or just think what has happened to tennis. Not too long ago there were only a few manufacturers like Wilson, Spalding, or Dunlop who put wooden racquets on the

4

market. Today there are at least ten times as many companies, each displaying a variety of models of different materials and compositions. In fact, each year brings a new batch of improved models reflecting the very latest scientific advancements. The same, of course, is true about warm-up suits, running shoes, hiking gear, diving equipment, fishing tackle, and so forth. You name it and they've got it in all sizes, shapes, and price ranges.

In the seventies, we went through several years when it was very much in vogue to look "leisurely" and the world of fashion was dominated by "leisure suits" which replaced the traditional suit and sport jacket. There is no doubt in my mind that people have been reached by recreation, or to be more precise, by the commercialization of recreation. Everybody is outfitted to the hilt and labeled with emblems and endorsements like a racing car or a professional athlete. No one needs to be alerted to what Nike, O.P. Adidas, and Lightning Bolt have meant to the California fashion scene. Labels reflecting *in* manufacturers, many of which are linked to the professional sports scene or connect the wearer to a specific sports lifestyle, are worn on shirts, scrawled down the sleeve, tacked to the pocket, tabbed on the side, embroidered on collars, printed into buttons, and silkscreened across fronts and backs. Then there are the telltale logos sewn, tacked, molded, printed, embroidered on shorts, pants, skirts, shoe backs, tongues, sides, soles, across visors and sweatbands, knitted into socks, engraved on sunglasses, watch faces and jewelry, not to mention the equipment totes. We, the recreation consumers, have become billboards, advertisements for the exploding recreational commercialism. We have swallowed the commercial bait—hook, line, and sinker. Recreation has developed into a sleeping giant.

2

Tomorrow's Generation Needs You

Recreation has grown into a giant, all right. But why a sleeping one, you might ask. The answer is very clear to me. Superficially, we are going through the motions in a grandiose style. But in the process, we have failed to incorporate the very essence of recreation into our way of life. We are in danger of completely losing the feeling for the experience that caused the leisure explosion to begin with. I am talking about that special attitude you recognize within yourself when you are recreating, when you are truly *at leisure*. You probably can't explain it, but I am sure you know when you have it and when you don't. When you do have it, you express it and sense it all over. It's a very special way of doing whatever you are doing. I call it *Recreative Lifestyle Attitude*. Having a recreative lifestyle attitude is being at leisure. Being at leisure is the very essence of recreation.

Now let me ask you a question: Has this recreative lifestyle attitude infiltrated the lives of people to the same extent that the commercialization has? I don't know about you, but for me, the answer is a very definite no. On the basis of my personal observation, the general lifestyle patterns of people can best be described by such words as hectic, frantic, restless, depressed, anxious, impatient, withdrawn, bored, or overly critical. Or, to put it differently, most of the time they are not relaxed, not easygoing, not playful, not without worry, not *not* in a hurry, and rarely ever lost in the moment.

When I talk about "lifestyle attitude," I am including not only all kinds of ways of making a living, but also such activities as playing golf, working in the yard, going on a trip, or reading the newspaper. Most people when they claim to be at leisure, change only location and equipment but not their basic attitude. They participate in so-called recreation activities, visit recreation facilities, wear recreation attire, and use the latest recreation gear. What is missing, of course, is their ability to recreate, to be at leisure, to have a recreative lifestyle attitude. They still are restless when vacationing, anxious when playing golf, or depressed when left to entertain themselves. Nevertheless, we have proudly announced the arrival of the leisure age, call it improving the quality of life and consider it progress. But like so many other developments that we have labeled progress in the past, this one too is mere self-deception. We are kidding ourselves. Recreation cannot be evaluated merely by concentrating on outward manifestations. Just as the number of people going to church or the amount of money earned from selling Bibles is no indication of a truly religious society. Religious attitude, like recreative lifestyle attitude, permeates all phases of human life, outside as well as inside of people, in their actions and in their awareness. Kneeling and folding the hands is not necessarily an indication of praying. A person also has to feel like praying. In other words, too many people just "go through the motions." They are "doing all the right things" but their hearts are not in it. For recreation, this would mean that they are demonstrating leisure behavior without really being at leisure.

The giant is sleeping indeed. Recreation has not yet reached the lives of people. Most of them are unable to experience a truly recreative lifestyle attitude, and lack a basic understanding of the importance of recreation for a modern society. This fact is demonstrated by the reaction of the public to critical issues that directly influence the quality of its lifestyle. Let me give you a couple of examples.

In the political arena, tax reform laws are sweeping the country. Infamous is California's pace-setting Proposition 13 which offered an overtaxed public immediate relief from the insatiable glut of

7

property taxes. The voting public welcomed Prop 13 with open arms. However, nothing comes from nothing and in order to balance a state budget which had been relieved of major incoming revenue in property taxes, cuts had to be made. And where were government cuts made in the leisure-prone society of populous California? Precisely in those areas where the public needed more funding, not less: in elementary and high schools, in colleges and universities, in police and public safety programs, and in parks and recreation departments.

Schools, which before were financially dependent on property tax revenues were forced to cut music, drama, dance, creative writing, athletics, and other elective programs, in order to subsist during the lean times of the post Prop 13 era. Ironically, these types of programs are the ones that prepare the young generation to face the ever-changing, leisure-oriented future world. Besides, they provide for personal growth experiences, and uphold all those values identified by society as desirable criteria for being more highly civilized.

Dwindling state budgets, reduced Parks and Recreation funding and communities were forced to cut staff and programs and to charge fees. Hardest hit by this squeeze were programs dealing with youth, older adults, and handicapped populations. Ironically, these groups need more recreation opportunities instead of less, as do elementary school children.

It has always surprised me that only very limited recreation programs for young children are provided. In as rich a country as ours, there are hardly any schools that have properly trained personnel or adequate facilities for recreation. It is in these formative years when the seeds for heathful lifestyle habits must be planted. During this time, children learn more easily than at any other period of their lives how good it feels to be active and healthy. If they become "movement addicts" early, they will benefit from it as long as they live. This is the reason why elementary schools need to employ qualified recreators, and to upgrade their facilities, programs, and attitudes toward recreation.

The situation is substantially better for secondary schools except that too much emphasis is placed on competition and winning. Ironically, as students get older, colleges and universities provide even better programs and have superior facilities and equipment. It is quite ridiculous, however, to make physical activity programs

8

mandatory at this point. By this time it is too late, and young men and women should not only have their own choice but should already be "hooked" on the need to move and recreate. Furthermore, where institutions of higher learning really fail is in preparing students for the leisure society that is with us already. They still refuse to include courses which deal with challenges of recreation and leisure into their general education requirements.

These are just a few examples to illustrate the general ignorance about recreation. I am sure you can add some more of your own. In any case, one thing becomes very clear: Before the leisure age can truly be announced, the general public's consciousness toward recreation has to be raised. This book is one attempt to do just this. After you have read it, I hope you will join the forces and spread the word. Tomorrow's generation needs you!

3

Let's Get Back to the Basics

The general public, as I have pointed out, does not understand the meaning and the importance of recreation. But, what is even more discouraging, is that many recreators themselves, when asked about the values of their own field, have difficulty giving a halfway satisfactory explanation. I am sure quite a few of you have raised the question yourself or have been asked by others. What is your answer? The response I get most of the time is something like this: "Well, Bruno, you know, I like working in recreation, and I really like the people I get involved with, and I like what they are doing. I also like playing and having fun with older people or with children. Besides, recreation is good for you." This is about all they could tell me. They never could really put their finger on anything special about recreation. At best, I was quoted some esoteric definitions from one of those unreadable textbooks. But it was immediately obvious that they had problems identifying with what the authors were trying to say. They didn't own their thoughts, and as a result, nobody, including me, could understand the meaning of their definitions. Consequently, they were unable to share with others what they felt so deeply about recreation.

Where there is a lack of understanding, there usually is doubt.

And where there is doubt, there is loss of cohesiveness. This is definitely true about recreation professionals. They are splitting into different interest groups and pulling in many directions. And what is most frightening is that out of their own ignorance they readily give up the very basic principles of recreation to fit the needs of others who are in more powerful positions, and who equally have no idea of what recreation is all about. The profession, as a result, is ripped into pieces, leaving its members without a unifying core. The situation reminds me of the words of William Butler Yeats in "The Second Coming":

> "The falcon cannot hear the falconer;
> Things fall apart; the center cannot hold."

Many recreators have lost their faith in recreation and are leaving the field like rats abandoning a sinking ship. Others are in danger of losing touch with the very essence of recreation – with what recreation is all about. This identity crisis is demonstrated in many different ways. Educators continue their search for new names for their departments in order to gain academic respectability. The truth is, they are unable to demonstrate to their colleagues what their field has to offer, not only to their institutions but to society in general. Recreators who serve special populations are readily giving up the intrinsically therapeutic and preventive power of recreation in exchange for techniques and treatment objectives that might earn them acceptance within medical hierarchies. Administrators are preoccupied with management issues and find themselves out of touch with principles of recreation that should be central to their work. No wonder they are unable to convince their city government and citizens alike that recreation is not a discretionary but an essential service for the people of their community. Outdoor recreators are in the process of shifting the emphasis of park services from natural resources to urban settings. They are overpowered by the politics involved, and in danger of losing it all. Commercial recreation operates strictly under profit-oriented merchant values, and is in desperate need for the type of input only true recreation professionals can provide.

What can recreators do to turn these values around? My advice to them is simply to go back to the basics. Go back to recreation! Quit trying to fit into the scheme of other fields. You will never gain recognition this way. The medium of recreation is recreation, not counseling, psychology, administration, horticulture, business, or any other field. Recreators have to rid themselves of their insecurities. They have to regain their belief in the values of recreation that attracted them to the field to begin with. They have to look at themselves and reestablish a solid feeling for who they are rather than be obsessed by who they think they should be, or what others expect them to be. Recreators have to make an all-out effort to redefine the fundamental principles of recreation. They need to communicate these principles in different languages in order to reach as many people as possible. Some presentations should be sophisticated enough to capture the attention of academicians, but others should be simplistic enough to make sense to the man on the street. What do you think gives recreation its uniqueness? How would you sell recreation to a city manager, a manufacturer, a physician, a friend...? Do you think the existence of recreation as a profession is justified? On what grounds? Is recreation scientifically founded? What special dimensions can recreation add to institutional settings?

In the following pages I will attempt to isolate some of the principles that give recreation its uniqueness. Let's go back to the basics.

4

The Wholeness of the Person

Since I hardly spoke English when I immigrated to the United States, I had never heard the word *recreation*. As a matter of fact, I didn't use the word until I began to study for my American doctorate at the University of Colorado in 1958. Though recreation was not a part of my vocabulary until then, I was very much aware of its meaning and the values associated with it. From a practical and conceptual point of view, my involvement with recreation goes back to my student days at the University of Vienna. It was during my early professional training in the late forties that I first became aware of the powerful attitude that permeates typical recreation settings. I began to discover the inherent pedagogic, therapeutic, and preventive forces of the recreation process. Since then I have incorporated this process into my approach in working with people and helping them to help themselves.

Let me tell you a story of how I first became aware of recreation. In 1946, right after World War II, I entered the University of Vienna and began to take courses dealing with general health, physical activity, and clinical psychology. From the beginning of my career I was interested in the well-being of the whole person. During the course of my studies I did part of my internship at the

Orthopedic Institute of Vienna. A large percentage of the patients were amputees who arrived in those early postwar years from all over Europe to seek help. The director of the institute was a very talented orthopedic surgeon of international reputation. He had worked for three years behind the lines in a M*A*S*H-type setting. It was true—war *is* hell. Injured men came from the battlefield to him with their heads literally under their arms. There were no insurance people looking over his shoulder when he operated. On top of all this, he was an extremely talented and sensitive man—a really exceptional person. Without a doubt, he picked up more experience in those three years than he could have gathered in three normal lifetimes. So, amputees flocked to him from all over Europe and other places around the globe, wherever there were people who needed his competencies. He operated, made skin grafts, shortened stumps, and did all the things that were necessary to fit prostheses properly. But, he soon found out that after all the medical procedures had been accomplished, there was another dimension he could not reach. And this dimension was to assist his patients in finding their way back to the routines of everyday living. He recognized the need for it but personally couldn't do anything about it, mainly because of his position. Being the director of the institute and a famous surgeon, patients would not allow him to come close to them. You see, Austria is still a rather traditional country, where some people have long titles to their names and where authority is still highly respected. So, whenever he tried to help his patients with some of their personal problems, they couldn't let him get close. His authority and the division of their social position stood between them. Whenever he asked a patient how he was doing, the patient clammed up, or politely dismissed the subject. In an atmosphere like this, it was impossible to accomplish anything. Besides, he also didn't have enough time for this type of work. So he asked the department of psychology at the University of Vienna if they could find two interns who would come over and help his patients. I was one of the two interns. I soon learned to give massages and to administer all kinds of physical therapy. During these treatment routines, I was asked to help patients psychologically with their problems of living.

At this stage of rehabilitation, physical medicine became rather superfluous. The emphasis shifted to other, more pertinent processes, and treatment activities served as a vehicle only. While

I massaged a young man who had lost both legs, I asked what he was going to do once he got out of here. "What can a crippled person do?" was his response. From then on, after the initial contact was made, we began to talk about all kinds of things, from war experiences to career plans and from everyday happenings to serious personal problems. During this time we also got involved in a variety of other activities. One day, I took him to a large public swimming pool. For the first time since he was injured, he eased himself into the water and discovered that he still could swim. The joy was written all over him. He told me later that first he had the feeling the whole world was looking at him. But, as time went on, he realized how other people were too busy with their own lives to pay attention to him. At the same time, one of the nurses and I used to take two arm amputees out for lunch and to the movies. At first, they found the world out there very threatening. They relied heavily on the relationship we had built up among us, using it as a kind of crutch while testing themselves and their surroundings. And usually, in practically all cases, the leisurely pace of massaging, swimming, eating, and having fun with friends began to take over. You could watch them becoming more relaxed, and above all, forgetting about themselves and what was missing in their lives.

It was in those days that I realized how important the process of recreation is to all people. Not only amputees have missing parts in their lives. We all do. We fragment our existence and become preoccupied with one aspect of it. The classical medical model, of course, uses the "missing part" approach almost exclusively and most of the time for very good reasons. Most professionals in the field of medicine have become highly specialized and concentrate their efforts on parts of the organism only. Ophthalmologists treat eyes, cardiologists work with the heart, urologists deal with the kidney and the bladder, dentists look after teeth, occupational therapists rehabilitate the part needed to return to work, and so forth. As a result of such specialization, the missing or defective part becomes the focal point. Consequently, what is left, or what is functioning – in this case, the rest of the person – tends to be ignored. Recreators recognize this problem, and refuse to let whatever is missing, abnormal, sick, or wrong take precedence over the holistic integrity of the individual. The wholeness of the person is central to the process of recreation.

15

5

On Bonding and Touching

The process of recreation provides unlimited opportunities for people to have fun together, to learn to know each other, to touch and be touched. Every time you are in a situation like this, wherever it might be—at home, at work, with friends or any group—before you are even aware of it, something very special happens. You begin to open up toward others and they in turn open up toward you. You allow yourself to come closer to somebody and allow somebody to come closer to you. You actively participate in what I call the process of *bonding*. I don't quite know how the whole thing develops, but I definitely recognize it when it is there and when it isn't. I also have found out that any type of activity can lead to bonding and that a truly recreative milieu is the ideal atmosphere for it to happen.

Once, very early in my career, I worked with a group of adolescents. All of them had been in trouble with the law in one way or another. During the course of the recreation program, we swam together, we wrestled, we played soccer, we talked very seriously at times, and we also had lots of fun. Within a relatively short period and without really trying, a very special relationship had developed between us. The young men accepted me, trusted me, and eventually shared with me some of their most cherished secrets. The human bond between us became a solid foundation not only for their personal growth but also for mine. We didn't have to analyze each other. Our relationship was real and alive. We lived it every day.

If I could single out one important feature with respect to bonding, it would have to be touching. I have seen this over and over again. We all need to be touched. Several years ago when I used to work with older adults in the San Francisco area, I had the capable assistance of a woman in her late seventies who was very active in our program. She related this story to me which well illustrates the need for touching:

> The other day when we visited the retirement home on Center Avenue, an older lady was sitting almost completely hidden in a corner. While most of the other women in the room were chatting with each other and asking me all kinds of questions about our program, she remained extremely withdrawn. After I had talked to all the other people, I walked over to her and asked how things were going. She responded with an empty and forlorn look. Then it came to my attention that her fingernails and cuticles were in very bad condition and that a lot of rough skin on her fingers was starting to break open. So I reached for my handbag and took out my manicure set. I took her left hand and began to cut her fingernails and snip off some of the hard skin particles around her fingertips. As I did this, I asked her a few questions directly related to what I was doing like, "Does this hurt you? Do you want me to do the other hand?" And this is when she said her first words, "Yes, please." This is how our conversation started. She began to tell me how thankful she was to me for doing this for her. After I had finished I took some cream out of my handbag and began massaging her hands. This is when I really experienced the first emotional reaction in her. Her face became flushed. She began to sit up a little bit straighter, and I recognized the strange mixture of upcoming tears and a certain delight in her eyes. She said that I really had been the first person in a long time to touch her in this way, by massaging her hands. She had forgotten how good it felt and how much she needed to be touched by another person.[3]

17

Touching plays a very important role in creating trusting and caring relationshps. In the story above, the cutting of the fingernails became one of the vehicles for the process of bonding and, as such, a recreative activity. This doesn't mean that we now have found a "fingernail cutting technique." On the contrary. There is no special way, no specific technique for achieving similar results. As a matter of fact, the activity as such is incidental. What is essential, though, is the presence of a truly recreative lifestyle attitude without goals, demands or expectations and one in which human beings can blossom and bonding can take place.

6

The Medium is Recreation

The word *recreation* is really a very beautiful word. It is defined in the dictionary as "the process of giving new life to something, of refreshing something, of restoring something." This something, of course, is the whole person. One refreshes the human organism in its totality by restoring its strength and its spontaneity. When you recreate, you recharge yourself and you actively participate in your own well-being. You say "yes" to life. You go with health. Consequently, the process of recreation is essentially "healthy" and as such is intrinsically therapeutic and preventive. In contrast, most people associated with the medical establishment are not going *with* health but rather *against* disease. They concentrate their work on disorders and the respective treatment modalities. What is *wrong* with a person remains central to their approach. In recreation, on the other hand, you support everything that is *right* within the lifestyle pattern of an individual and thereby contribute to his general well-being. It is this approach that separates recreation from all other helping professions.

The failure to understand and apply this difference in philosophy has had many unfortunate results. A perfect example is the progressive trend of separating therapeutic recreation from the rest of the field. For many therapeutic recreation specialists, it seems to be more important to be identified as a treatment expert than a recreator. In their ignorance they sacrifice the whole for the part. The tail is wagging the dog. Furthermore, placing *therapeutic* in front of recreation is a prolixity, a superfluous repetition. Recreation *is* therapeutic. Both words say the same, and the additional word in front does not add anything. Recreation, above all, is recreation. It is not something that can be cut into pieces. Either you are recreating or you are not. Where, how, and with whom you are at leisure is completely secondary.

"Recreation for special populations" is another one of those meaningless terms. What does it mean? Are there populations that are not as special, unspecial, or nonspecial? Again, let us not forget that we are dealing with people and all people are able to recreate. If they have one arm, if they have diabetes, if they have a bad heart, if they have mental problems, if they are retarded, that has nothing to do with their ability to recreate. Where, how, and who is recreating does not change the process of recreation. The term *special population* in this sense is directly opposed to the concept of *mainstreaming*. To differentiate between old and young or sick and healthy is outright prejudice and not important as far as a person's recreative lifestyle attitude is concerned. It is just as absurd as making a distinction between the recreation of blacks and whites, gays and straights, or men and women. People are people. And, if you look closely enough, all of us can be put into one special population or another. You are a human being and all human beings have the need and the capacity to develop a recreative lifestyle attitude. It's as simple as that.

The present model implies that just because you're old, sick, or blind, you must be engaged in recreation for special populations and not simply recreation. Or just because you are labeled schizophrenic, you are doing therapeutic recreation instead of plain recreation. This is crazy. The only legitimate reason for exchanging therapeutic recreation for recreation is for the establishment and survival of recreation in medical, paramedical, and other institutionalized settings where the true values of recreation are not understood. In these situations I personally prefer the term recreation therapy. My interpretation of recreation therapy is recreation as therapy. Important is the realization that the word "therapy" is used only as a crutch in order to gain acceptance among people who don't know very much about recreation to begin with. They are the ignorant ones. If you work with other professionals you should never give up your own identity in exchange for procedures and theories that belong to other specialties. But, you should learn as much as possible about those other fields in order to be able to explain to people in their own language what recreation is all about.

Students who are preparing to work in specialized settings are required to study medical terminology and pathology along with other subject matter more closely related to their field. The reason for including this material in their curriculum is to enable them to function effectively by knowing the jargon everyone is using. It is definitely not taught to make little doctors out of them, to diagnose and to treat illnesses or to administer purposive intervention as it is often stated in high-flying terms. In order to get accepted into any group, you have to be able to speak and understand the language of that group. Or as Caesar once said, "Know the language of your enemy." If you don't, you will remain an outsider, mistrusted and misunderstood, and you will be unable to infiltrate any existing structure.

Once you have managed to become a valuable member of a group, you can begin to educate everyone around you. As a recreator you then must demonstrate what you and your field have to offer and convince the people you come in contact with of the values of your discipline. You must help them understand that recreation operates under completely different principles from most of the other helping professions. You need to explain to them that by catering to their philosophy, you would have to give up the very essence of what recreation can contribute to their agency. You must make them understand that this difference is the strength of recreation, not its weakness. Slowly but surely your superiors will gain more insight into what you are doing and what your basic tenets are.

Once you demonstrate competency in their language, you will gain their confidence and their support. Then you can begin to explain in your language the unique contribution recreation can make to their institution. You can convince them that what you are doing has to be completely different from their treatment approach. If you are forced into the same professional framework they are operating within, it will destroy the very essence of what recreation has to offer to institutionalized settings. Dr. Paul Haun,[4] a well-known physician, writes:

> Today the recreation worker is the only member of the treatment, health or rehabilitation team who can make the patient's healthy psychologic needs his sole exclusive concern. This is far more than providing a place for the patient to go during the hours he is not "needed" in therapy. And, to be both honest as well as effective, it must not in my view serve as a subterfuge for some disguised and unspoken purpose. All patients, and particularly psychiatric patients, are in desperate need of getting away, on occasion, from the stare of clinical appraisal – of being able to do something with another person, of talking to a friend, of silently sharing the warmth of companionship – without fear of being booby-trapped into a clinically significant admission.

The trend of more and more recreators getting away from the essential ingredients of recreation is very disturbing. They are insecure about their field and overwhelmed by the "clean-cut" procedures of their colleagues. In their dilemma they adapt philosophies and practices that belong to other fields just to win "professional acceptance." A great deal of their time is spent with charting, behavior modification, assertiveness training, leisure counseling, and who knows what else. Recreation is sacrificed in exchange for activites which at best should only be peripheral to their program. This approach is not only self-defeating but, in the long run, self-destructing. Recreators, in order to survive as a profession and to fulfill their responsibilities toward society, have to remain true to themselves. The medium is recreation.

7

Being Scared to Death

Since I gave my first lecture some thirty years ago, I have done a lot of public speaking. Now, after all this time, I still get quite anxious when I step in front of people. My mouth gets dry, my legs feel a bit shaky, and I sense some tightness in my chest. In the beginning of my career as a lecturer, I used to fight these feelings and tell myself, "Come on, Bruno, pull yourself together." So I indeed pulled myself together, put my nose into my notes and made sure I didn't miss a word. As it turned out, I didn't even miss one letter, but I missed all the people. They fell asleep on me.

Nowadays, when I deliver a major address, I still get butterflies in my stomach but I allow myself to go *with* my anxiousness and share my feelings with the audience. At first, the quality of my voice is rather tentative; I stutter a little bit and my eyes search for early responses in people's faces. Then, after a relatively short time, I can actually feel myself making contact with others. I get a sense of who they are and they in turn begin to hear me. In order to reach this point and possibly even improve upon it, I have to give up some of the material I am presenting. But, in return for losing content, I gain the attention and participation of the people I am speaking to. I gladly make this exchange because I have learned to realize that a loss of material is much less important for the success of my presentation than the loss of the audience. In fact, the quality of the milieu which permeates the presentation actually *becomes* the presentation.

The quality of the milieu is made up of unlimited forces which in their totality give it its character. Most of these forces originate from highly complex processes and are impossible to isolate or specify. In scientific circles they are referred to as *nonspecific forces.*[5] I learned the importance of nonspecific forces when I worked at the Lovelace Foundation for Medical Education and Research. There I became involved in a research project which examined the reactions of the human organism to extreme heat.[6] For this purpose I acquired a sauna and made it possible to create an environment of over 200 degrees. The population for the experiment consisted of 25 physical education majors from the University of New Mexico. Prior to the actual testing procedure, all students underwent a medical examination and several pilot studies familiarized them with the hot room and the electronic measuring devices. I expected that these preliminary measures would eliminate undesired reactions. As it turned out, during the actual experiment, three subjects fainted and had to be removed from the sauna after three, four, and seven minutes respectively. Now, the interesting point is that the specific force of heat could not, after such a short time, have been the cause for the loss of consciousness. After only a few minutes, there simply is not enough stress on the circulatory system to affect a person physiologically. Something else must have taken place during the experiment. It was not the heat, the controlled variable, but uncontrolled nonspecific forces that caused these men to faint. In American colloquialism we have an expression for what happened. We say they "psyched themselves out." Personally, I don't like to use the word *psyche* because it gives the impression of having nothing to do with the body. Rather than the "psyche," I prefer to use the term *lifestyle attitude* and define it as a process which affects the whole organism, its thoughts, emotions, and actions. I would say that the lifestyle attitude of the participants in this experiment resulted from nonspecific forces originating from both the milieu to which they were exposed and from that which they created within themselves. It was the lifestyle attitude of the three subjects under investigation that fainted them.

The power of attitude has been recognized by many inves-

24

tigators. Walter B. Cannon,[7] the famous Harvard physiologist, looked into the question of voodoo death and tells a story of a young bushman who, deceived by a practical joke, ate a bird absolutely forbidden to his tribe. When he learned the "truth" and became aware that he had gone against a taboo, he died within 24 hours. Did the bird kill him? No, of course not. It was he himself who participated in the creation of a constellation of nonspecific forces, strong enough to kill him. He was "scared to death" by his attitude.

In another study,[8] a psychologist conducted a rather grim experiment with rats. First, he divided them into two groups. He took the first group and deposited them into a water tank from which they couldn't escape, thus forcing them to swim. He did exactly the same with the second group, except that he clipped their whiskers first. To make a long, rather grim story short, this group drowned in a much shorter time than the first one. If we examine the specific conditions for staying afloat, we end up with such things as specific weight, lung volume, muscular efficiency, or air bubbles caught in the fur. As you know, none of these variables were tampered with. The question we end up asking ourselves is: Do whiskers play a specific part in the process of keeping the rat above water? Of course they don't. Rats maintain their contact with the environment mainly through their whiskers. Clipping them affects their self-confidence, their ego. It changes their attitude from "fighting to the last moment" to one of "giving up earlier." The rats with clipped whiskers gave up and drowned much sooner. I am sure you all are familiar with the story of Samson. His long hair was a symbol of his strength. Delilah, by cutting his hair, destroyed his might and made his capture possible. Perhaps if you were to shave my head right now, I might not be able to utter another word.

The phenomenon of "giving up" is a well-documented fact in the field of gerontology. Anyone who has worked with older people knows it under the name of *marasmus*. A rather typical situation involving an older couple goes something like this: Both are in their late 70's and they have been married for fifty years. He has a long-standing ailment and finally dies of it. She is a healthy, energetic woman but a few months after her husband's death, she suddenly dies. An autopsy is performed and nothing wrong can be found, with her. All we can say is that she decided to die, so she died. The medical literature is full of reports of surgeons[9] refusing to operate on patients who are convinced they won't live through the operation. Physicians know from experience that with such an attitude, they won't. "Operation successful, patient dead" becomes a reality. Apparently, we all have the power of "being scared to death" by our own lifestyle attitude.

8

When Flowers Are Handled

Nonspecific forces are not of the unpleasant or threatening kind only; they come in all forms, intensities and qualities. They can kill you and make you sick, but they also have the power to work for you, to heal you, to prevent you from getting sick, or to promote your well-being. You can, in other words, develop lifestyle attitudes that are pleasant and life supporting. When I speak about developing a lifestyle attitude, I don't necessarily mean that you have full control over the way it expresses itself. As a matter of fact, most of the expressions, more often than not, originate without your conscious input. The most powerful ones become a part of you without you ever being aware of what happened to you. The old Chinese master Wu-tsu Fa-yen expressed this experience so beautifully in this poem:

> When water is scooped by the hands,
> the moon is reflected in them;
> When flowers are handled,
> the scent soaks into the robe.

Let's take those last two lines of the poem and pretend that you are a florist. You spend all day arranging the flowers and taking care of all the other responsibilities associated with your florist business. In the evening you come home tired, still lost in thought about your shop. At the door your little boy comes running toward you, gives you a big hug and says: "Gee, dad, you smell so good." In your preoccupation with your business you were totally unaware that the scent of the flowers was absorbed by your clothes. You didn't smell them any longer. Still, they became a part of you.

In our lives, we all have a tendency to be practically hypnotized by what we *think* we are doing, be it scooping up water, handling flowers, raising children, making a living, etc. We concentrate on the best way, the fastest way, and above all, the right way. In the process we are completely overwhelmed by our head trip and many significant happenings escape us completely. Another way of expressing the same idea is to say that "a person tends to pass on more of what he is, than what he knows." You, through your lifestyle attitude – that is, the milieu you create within and around yourself – continuously give off messages. These messages or "vibes" as they are referred to in the vernacular are very strong and subtly expressed in whatever you happen to do. You are transmitting yourSELF by osmosis, you might say. What you are preoccupied with, what you know, or what you *think* you are doing often gets lost in the process. Children are very good at picking up vibes. Many times they don't understand the meaning of your words, but they figure you out by the way you present your words. They sense you. Your lifestyle attitude gives you away.

When you interact with a milieu, your environment, you make adjustments in your inner milieu, your organism. If the adjustments are strong enough or persist long enough, they tend to become embodied in you. They become expressions of your lifestyle attitude; they become you. An environment, that is experienced by you as fear-arousing, for instance, will indeed make you fearful. If the situation persists, you will, sooner or later, develop a fearful attitude. You become a fearful person. What is equally important to realize is that by being fearful you can actively participate in creating a fear-arousing milieu.

The same principle holds true for recreation. The process of recreation is based both on the recreative lifestyle attitude of individuals and a recreative milieu. You participate in creating a recreative milieu by your ability to be at leisure. Consequently, you are assisted in developing your ability to be at leisure by a recreative milieu. The relationship between individuals and milieu is reciprocal. The strength of the process of recreation lies in the holistic character of this reciprocal relationship. Or as Wu-tsu Fa-yen has said, "When flowers are handled, the scent soaks into the robe."

9

Your Attitude Matters,
Not the Game

Recreation to most people is associated with all kinds of activities collectively known as arts, crafts, games, sports, relaxation, and pastimes. They range from hiking, singing, and swimming to meditating, praying, and breathing. I personally have used these and many other activities in working with people of all ages, in small or large groups, or on a one-to-one basis in my private practice. However, my attention was not focused on the activities per se, but on the attitude associated with them. I recognized that when you are recreating, you are at leisure and when you are truly at leisure, you have a recreative lifestyle attitude. It is this attitude that determines *how* you are actually doing an activity. And the *how* is much more important than the what. Are you uptight or relaxed? Do you have fun or is it a chore? The emphasis is on the underlying attitude and not on the activity. As a matter of fact, the activities most of the time are used only as a pretext for processes that might as well happen without their apparent involvement. Let me give you an illustration of what I mean. Recreators often are referred to as having an easy job. All they have to do is "throw out the ball." People who say this are, of course, unable to see beyond the actual ball game. They are unaware of the many things that go on after the ball has been thrown out. They don't see that the ball no longer is just a ball, but becomes an instrument responsible for a vast variety of happenings. Individuals involved in a ball game, are having a ball, are making friends, are laughing together, are losing themselves, are exercising their muscles, are releasing frustration, are gaining self-confidence, are saying "yes" to life, are being touched by others, are touching others themselves, are overcoming their shyness, and so forth. The list is endless. Suddenly, a ball game is no longer just a ball game, but is all the things I have listed and much more. Of course, conversely, individuals in a ball game who are not recreating, who only *think* they are, may not be having a ball at all. They can be making enemies, cursing and jeering at one another, tensing their muscles, compounding frustrations, losing self-confidence, counting the score, worrying about the performance of themselves, of their team, of the other team, their standing among other teams now and in the future. The list is endless. After the ball game is over, they are "wiped out" for hours afterwards as they relive what happened, what could have happened, what should have happened, and so forth.

Nowadays, people tend to think they are recreating when they watch professional sporting events. Many put undue meaning into these professional games. They live their lives surreptitiously through the lives of athletes. As unbelievable as it sounds, after the Super Bowl, some fans actually suffer withdrawal symptoms. Weekends become a burden, lose purpose and meaning, and leave them feeling aimless, bored, and depressed. In extreme cases, a few spectators actually experience grief syndromes just like those which accompany the death of a loved one.

Sitting in a chair, reading this, it may sound laughable or even preposterous. And definitely not everyone participates to this extreme in professional athletic events. However, the conditioning to become so involved in a game or a team starts very early in life. It may begin at seven or eight in youth sports such as Little League baseball or soccer. It continues through high school with logos and inspirationally named school teams; into colleges and universities; and then into cities where urban dwellers identify with their home town team. Ironically, the players themselves do not identify as strongly with their locale; most are content to move with the best contract. For them, "money talks."

Therefore, it becomes obvious that feelings of loyalty, of belonging, of love for the alma mater are at best temporary, and most probably, nonexistent. What they are, in reality, are emotional reactions to competitive settings without the active involvement. What they become are conditioned emotions by passive spectators —persons who have given up being active themselves and who instead have assumed a passive lifestyle. They give up their own life and invest their emotions surreptitiously in the lives of others—the team, the quarterback, the score, etc.

San Diego's well-known sportcaster, Ted Leitner, faced the six o'clock news viewers after the home town football team lost its bid to qualify for the Super Bowl and quipped, "Hey, it's only a game!" And for this phrase he is famous! Why? Because he captured the perspective of the issue and brought a tension-saturated, thoroughly depressed public back to reality. "Hey, it's only a game!" Super Bowls come and Super Bowls go. So do football teams. So do the fans. It's your attitude that matters, not the game.

10

How You Are Is What You Get

Recreation is a process characterized by a special attitude which I call recreative lifestyle attitude. If you have a recreative lifestyle attitude, you are at leisure. Being at leisure is a certain way of how you live your life. Do you resent having to cook or do you love cooking? Do you smile when in fact you are angry at your mother-in-law? Are you going to tell her the reasons for your anger? Chances are she senses anyhow that you resent her, smiling or no smiling. Your attitude is giving you away. Your whole person is permeated by the way you feel and how you do whatever you are doing. The way you smile and shout, move and breathe, think and metabolize — are all expressions of how you are on this earth.

You pay a different price for smiling while swallowing your anger than by openly expressing it. Your experience, or "what you get," is not only reflected in your environment, like the reactions of your mother-in-law, but is also expressed within yourself and through yourself in the form of motions, thoughts, dreams, muscle tensions, headaches, a raised blood sugar level, upset stomach, etc. All of these expressions are representative of different aspects of the same reality.

It is in this sense that I view the process of recreation or, more precisely, the intrinsic power of a recreative lifestyle attitude as a key to healthful living. I have discovered that when you are at leisure, you create a milieu which is conducive to a feeling of general well-being. When you are relaxed and not threatened by anything, you have a better chance of improving your self-confidence, of overcoming your timidity, of talking to people, of ridding yourself of tension, or of simply having fun. In order to decide whether or not an activity is recreative, it is not enough to merely analyze what someone is doing. Often, for instance, activities are referred to as leisure behavior, but when you take a closer look you will discover that the people involved are not behaving leisurely at all. And vice versa, you might consider a person to be "working" when in fact he is at leisure. The classical dualism and mutual exclusiveness of work and play no longer apply. The type of activity doesn't make the difference. What does make the difference is the underlying attitude.

This reminds me of a friend with whom I play golf regularly. He works in his dad's business and he loves it. There are a lot of congenial men and women in his office and they have a lot of fun together. He also is a coffee connoisseur. He brings the latest Colombian melange to the office and enjoys the ritual of making coffee. He enjoys the aroma and takes in the full scenery. When he goes to his desk to do his work, he loves it too. He is excited about it; he loses his sense of time; he is totally engrossed. He lives strictly in the here and now. That's the picture of how he *works.* Then he goes and *plays* golf with me. He kills himself playing golf. You can see the agony in his face and almost hear the acid burning holes into his stomach. What's happening in his life? Well, when he drinks his coffee, he is right there with it. He tastes, he smells, he sees, he works at his desk and he enjoys. His body and his awareness are both right there together in one piece. How about his golf? While he hits the ball, he is either reminiscing about the five iron he just hacked into the ground or he is anticipating his overall poor score. In other words, when he plays golf, his body is right here but his awareness is either in the past or the future. They are separated from each other. He can't "get it together."

Your body can only be in the present. It is at every moment of your life a part of the moment. Every breath you take, you take here and now. Your body IS. The place is here; the time is now. But it is different with your awareness. During most of your life,

34

your awareness is not in the present. Either you anticipate what might happen or you reminisce about what should have happened. Your head is in the future or the past. You worry about tomorrow. "If I don't pass the examination, I won't get the job." You lose Thursday anticipating Friday. "I can hardly wait until Friday when we'll be together again." The same is true about the past. "I should have told him off." "Why didn't I ask her when I had the chance?" "How could he do this to me?" In any case, your body is separated from your awareness. When you live exclusively this way, you not only miss out on the present, but eventually you create tension, anxiety and *dis-ease*. You become the victim of your lifestyle which is dominated by what I call your *Analytic Lifestyle Attitude*. When, on the other hand, you live your life in the present, you allow yourSELF to experience your life as it happens from moment to moment. You have your body and your awareness together. They form a whole – a *Gestalt*, as they say in German. Your lifestyle becomes enriched by your recreative lifestyle attitude.

A well-rounded lifestyle has a balance of recreative and analytic lifestyle attitudes just as the well-functioning organism vacillates between tension and relaxation. The problem with modern living is that it is almost totally analytic. Instead of dealing with at least half of our life in the here and now, you concern yourself almost exclusively with the future or the past, and thereby miss out on the moment. Nowadays we read a lot about lifestyle, but basically we are talking about analytic lifestyle attitude only. All we change is the activity, not the attitude. Modern man has almost completely lost touch with his recreative lifestyle attitude which is the very crux of his nature. Leisure is threatening to modern man. And most people think that by changing their activities, they will resolve their problem. But instead, they find themselves working as hard at play as they do at work. I'm sure you can think of someone who attacks his vacation in the same way he works all year. He probably races from city to city or freeway to freeway, meeting schedules and deadlines and missing it all in the process. It is his attitude that needs to change. In order to find true leisure, you must change the attitude beind your lifestyle. "How you are is what you get."

11

Being At Leisure
Is A Lifestyle Attitude

The analytic lifestyle attitude can be a positive force which enriches man's life. It employs the type of brain action that separates us from the rest of the animal world. By using a higher level of awareness, we have gained the ability to plan for the future and to learn from past experiences. It has enabled us to better the quality of our lives and to progress. But the same awareness level has also caused man considerable anguish. I am referring to what is known in medical terms as a mass discharge of the sympathetic nervous system. I call it the *crisis reaction*. It has a very important function in your life when you confront real conflict or danger. It prepares your body to take immediate action, enabling you to run away or attack. And, if it happens to be a false alarm, your organism automatically returns to its normal state. If a deer should hear a noise while grazing, it will raise up, its legs will stiffen, the ears will prick up and as the result of parasympathetic overcompensation, it will lose some urine and feces. If you could look inside the deer's body, you would detect certain blood flow patterns, reactions to adrenalin output, or a dryness of the mouth. If nothing happens, the system will return to normal and the deer will

36

resume its activity. You have the same built-in mechanism. But what differentiates you from the deer is that you also can create danger in your head that does not exist in reality. It exists in your head only and you can keep it there as long as you decide to, from a couple of minutes to a lifetime. You anticipate what could happen if... but your body can't act on it. It can ony react to your headtrip. In its natural function, the crisis reaction is of very short duration. It prepares you to act. The activated energy is discharged immediately through your action. The headtrip, on the other hand, can continue for prolonged periods of time. You anticipate and anticipate and anticipate and your body reacts and reacts and reacts, but you never act. Some people live their whole lives like this. Their energy is blocked and they experience constant tension.

You can get a pretty good feeling for the crisis reaction by pretending to be suddenly surprised by a dangerous situation. To illustrate this right now, act very startled—as though you were pantomiming a frightening situation. Now get in touch with what happens to your body. The first reaction you probably become aware of is that you suck air in and stop breathing. Your shoulders are pulled up and you are probably up on your toes with your pelvis rigid and your legs stiff. What happens to you if this crisis reaction continues for a prolonged period of time, when general body tension turns into a chronic state? Your brows are pulled together. The muscles of your eyes and forehead are tight. Your eyes are wide open and pupils are dilated. There's a worried look on your face. Your tongue is coated. Your mouth is dry and your lips pursed. You feel a tenseness in your jaws as though you had a lump in your throat. You are choking. The muscles of your neck and throat are tense. You are holding on to your breath or are breathing shallowly. The emphasis is on inhalation which is the first sign of wanting to control the situation. Holding your breath gives you a false feeling of control and power. Instead you only make your chest immobile and pull your shoulders up. Your arms assume a defensive position. Your hands are overextended and cold and sweaty. Your pelvis is rigid. Your anus is pulled in. You are up on your toes. Your genitals are contracted. You are up and tight. Uptight—the word expresses it precisely.

What is showing on the outside of your body is only the result of what is going on inside of you. Your larynx tightens up. You can

37

hear it by the way you speak and breathe. Your blood vessels are constricted and your heart rate is increased. Your blood pressure rises. Your adrenal cortex reacts with oversecretion and initiates continuous hypertension. This way, even without actual stress, you keep your blood pressure up, produce chronic muscular tension and upset your blood sugar level. The spasm of the sphincter muscles of your stomach keeps air from passing through. The air starts to collect and your stomach balloons. Your heart is pushed up. You feel pressure on your heart and butterflies in your stomach. Because your heart is pushed up, the left side of your lungs is compressed. You feel pain and tension on your left side. Your diaphragm is raised and rigid and cannot function freely. Your breathing is shallow. The tightening of your anus causes constipation and hemorrhoids. The increased acidity in your stomach initiates peptic ulcers. The tenseness in your jaw makes you grind your teeth at night. Your overworked head answers with a migraine. You are one big mass of blocked energy. You are in pain. You are hurting.

What can you do to escape this dilemma? The usual way to get out from under this hypertense and anxiety-ridden state is to reach for booze or drugs, or to simply fall apart. After a few drinks you've eliminated all senstions of tension by knocking yourself out. You're collapsed. But neither in the state of hypertension nor in the state of collapse are you really relaxed. Both conditions keep you from experiencing your body, your *self*. Your senses are dulled and distorted. You *think* you are recreating, when in fact you are far removed from having a recreative lifestyle attitude.

Treating the symptoms of an abortive lifestyle can bring only temporary relief. If your attitude is wrong, you are living poorly and are paying a high price for it. The crisis reaction and your extra level of consciousness, which nature designed to protect you, become your worst enemies. What you have to change is your way of living. You have to rediscover your recreative lifestyle attitude and counterbalance your overextended analytic lifestyle attitude with it. Only in this way will you be able to improve the quality of your life. The process of recreation is essential to healthful living. Being at leisure is a lifestyle attitude.

12

You Are Your Attitude

An essential part of how you live is determined by an all-pervasive milieu which surrounds you from the moment of birth and maybe even earlier than that. Before you are grown up enough to ask the question, "Who am I?" you are *you* already. And by being who you are, you help maintain the very thing that made you to begin with. This is the main reason that it is so difficult to bring about change on the human scene. Once a groove has been cut into your brain or, more correctly, into your whole organism, it is very difficult to alter it. You end up experiencing and reacting to the world around you in a very specific way and thereby, you not only maintain this well-established pattern, but participate in passing it on to others.

Still, times do change and so do people. Different periods in the history of mankind have used different frames of reference concerning how to view the world. It was Goethe who originated the term *Zeitgeist* which literally translated means the spirit of a specific time in history—its attitude. What we nowadays call "consciousness raising" is just another expresson for a change in Zeitgeist—in how you change your attitude toward certain aspects of life. For instance, you only have to go back a few years and you will find hardly a single newspaper article about the plight of women or older people. These issues hadn't reached the consciousness of society yet and, therefore, were not a part of its Zeitgeist. They were not in vogue. Twenty years ago we saw women in a different way—as homemakers and childrearers—certainly not how we see them today.

This reminds me of an incident when I first arrived on the North American continent in the fall of 1954. I was picked up in Toronto by an old friend of my father who sponsored my immigration to Canada. He was the owner of the Toronto Maple Leafs ice hockey team. After he picked me up from the ship, we drove from the harbor in Montreal directly to a hockey game at the Maple Leaf Garden in Toronto. As I looked around at the spectators, I was surprised to see numerous white-haired older women in pastel hats and coats, knitting and following the game enthusiastically. In Austria, where I came from, women, after the age of 50, dressed "their age." They wore dark colors: black, gray, navy, and brown. They certainly were not competitive sports fans. The society they grew up in thought old and so they lived old! After I had lived for a couple of years in North America, I observed older adults actively involved in many facets of Canadian and American life. I liked what I saw. They lived a vital existence, calling their own shots, free from preconceived ideas of how older adults are supposed to think and act. A lot has happened since 1955 to the lifestyle attitude of older people regarding their feelings toward themselves and society's attitude toward them. The whole revolution of older adults has made a lasting impact on our society.

And yet, any revolution or form of change, even a change for the better, can be very threatening to people in general. A change in fashion, such as the length of skirts or hair, can be as upsetting as the declaration that the earth is no longer the center of the universe. Of course, the things that make some people afraid and uptight, attract and relax others. Kwang-tse, the Chinese sage, has an interesting way of saying just that:

> A beautiful woman who gives pleasure to men
> serves only to frighten fish
> when she jumps into the water.

You might say: Different features for different creatures.

As you get older, you change the way you look at yourself and the things around you. You see yourself and your parents quite differently at 15 than you do at 25 or 55. Some lifestyle attitudes, however, never change, and you hold on to them for one reason or another. Being conservative, liberal, progressive, or radical are aspects of a personal lifestyle attitude just as being uptight, relaxed, angry, cynical, or anxious are.

The term Zeitgeist usually has a historical connotation. It is used mainly to characterize a certain period of history. But lifestyle attitude, as I use the expression, goes much deeper. It penetrates the skin. Lifestyle attitude, as I refer to it in this book, encompasses the whole organism and its interaction with the environment. In other words, your lifestyle attitude is not only in your head, but is embodied in you by the way you stand, move, breathe and metabolize, tense and relax, dream and perceive, learn and teach, and interact with your surroundings. Your personal lifestyle attitude is the true expression of how you live and consequently of who you are. You *are* your attitude.

13

Being Cool Is The Message

What is true about your own attitude is also true about the collective lifestyle attitude of a whole society. Societies differ from each other in very much the same way as you differ from me. Different groups of people develop different ways of living. For some, tomorrow is central to their lives; for others there is no tomorrow.

Nonliterate societies, for example, relate to the world on a strictly experiential level. Modern societies, on the other hand, deal with people and objects more symbolically by assigning names to them. Consequently, the way they experience their world is dominated by the words they use to describe it. For instance, the moment one finds out what a man's occupation is, he is identified by the name of his occupation and no longer is an individual person. He becomes *the* mechanic, *the* doctor, *the* policeman, or *the* English teacher. An English teacher is the person in front of an English class. He is expected only to pass on what he knows about English and the student, in turn, is supposed to absorb only what he is passing on.

Do you believe this? I don't. I know from my own experience that my best teachers were the ones that were special individuals. They passed on more to me by what they were as persons than by what they knew. The subject matter content became secondary in the learning experience. John Miller, English teacher, does not teach English half as much as he teaches John Miller. And if John Miller gains your respect and admiration as a person, I guarantee that he will win you over to English as well. This concept is difficult to perceive for educators who deal with learning strictly in terms of educational objectives that are closely tied to their subject matter content. The word *content* reminds me of a story told in Austria about a tool factory. In hopes of reducing employee theft, all workers were searched regularly upon leaving their job site. Every day one worker had his wheelbarrow inspected before carting it off the premises. Nothing was ever found. The worker, of course, was stealing the wheelbarrows. The inspector, in his preoccupation with looking for content, overlooked the container.

The same idea has been expressed by the spokesman of the electronic age, Marshall McLuhan,[10] with his famous phrase "the medium is the message." For McLuhan it is the container not the content that is important. It is the person and not what he is saying. In the same vein, for most of us, a car is a means of transportation. It gets us from point A to point B. That's about it. But for McLuhan, the car is directly responsible for breaking up families, for separating work and home, for exploding cities into suburbs, for creating asphalt jungles, and for wrecking railroads. The medium indeed is the "massage,"[11] as he punned in a later book.

McLuhan[12] also makes a special effort to point out that it is television as such and not the program that has a major impact on society. TV for him is an all-involving sensory experience which he contrasts with the strictly visual demand of print. The onlooker becomes totally absorbed by television. Television virtually touches the viewer. In contrast, the written word isolates the reader from the rest of the world. McLuhan insists that "tactility could only have been lost to human awareness in a visual culture which is dissolving under the impact of electric circuitry." Television for him is directly responsible for helping modern man to enrich his limited visual experience of the world by rediscovering the other senses. Did the need for touching regain importance through the medium of television? Are sensitivity training sessions and all those "touchy-feely" workshops that sprang up in the sixties signs of conquest over the printed word?

Any medium, according to McLuhan, can be hot or cool. For

him, "A hot medium allows for less participation than a cool one, as a lecture makes for less participation than a seminar, and a book for less than a dialogue." For him, "Hot media are, therefore, low in participation, and cool media are high in participation or completion by the audience." He further stresses that ". . .it makes all the difference whether a hot medium is used in a hot or a cool culture. The hot radio medium used in cool or nonliterate cultures has a violent effect, quite unlike its effect, say in England or America, where radio is considered entertainment. A cool or low literacy culture cannot accept hot media like movies or radio as entertainment. They are, at least, as radically upsetting for them as the cool TV medium has proven to be for our high literacy world."

Expanding on this idea, recreation too could be identified as a cool medium. The process of recreation, after all, has relatively low visual orientation and calls for a high degree of completion by its participants. A *focused* treatment procedure differs from a *diffused* recreative milieu in very much the same way as a lecture differs from a seminar. Could it be that our hot analytic culture experiences a similar problem with recreation as it does with TV? Modern man apparently needs to learn to incorporate cool media into his lifestyle. The best way might be to first of all cool himself off by adopting a recreative lifestyle attitude. For modern man, being cool, that is, being at leisure is the message.

14

Step To A Different Drummer

The concept that an individual, a television set, a car or any "medium" can mean different things to different people has found expression in other areas of human interest. In the field of anthropology, for instance, it was discovered that Eskimos can decipher maps and pictures from any angle. To the Eskimo there is no right-side-up or up-side-down. They can draw as well looking down as they can lying on their back looking up or sitting in front and drawing horizontally. Because their world is white-on-white, they live without linearity. To compensate for their nonlinear environment, they have developed fantastic memories. Living in a white, snow-covered world, they have created fifty words for "snow." Snow to them is central to their life and as varying as flavors of ice cream to us. Eskimos absorb all the nuances, the distinct characteristics of different types of snow. It becomes important how they see snow, not what they see. Consequently, their way of perceiving the world is different from other cultures' way of perceiving the world.[13]

In the same respect, it took my wife and me, who came from seasonal climates, years to adjust to the moderate "sameness" of Southern California. "Don't you get sick of all the warm weather and sun? Isn't it boring after a while?" our friends and relatives from the north would ask. Of course it wasn't "the same" or boring day after day once we tuned in to the subleties of California climate. Just as the Ekimos have fifty words for "snow," Californians have numerous ways of describing "warm and sunny," depending on winds, desert conditions, coastal variation, cloud formations and, unfortunately, smog conditions.

Each society outfits its members with glasses that have very specific lenses in them. These lenses determine *how* they see and *what* they see. This can be very clearly demonstrated in the animal world. In a study by Konrad Lorenz[14] involving water shrews, he discovered that although their eyes are fully developed and they can see very well, they rely almost entirely on their sense of smell to get around and explore their environment. In a strange environment, shrews will repeat the trip over and over again always using the same jagged path. It never occurs to any of them to use their eyes and *see* that the shortest distance between two points is a straight line. Although their eyes were developed to see, seeing was overruled by smelling and sensing with whiskers. Naturally, this unconscious choice of olfactory over visual input influences the shrews' perception of the world. The shrew exchanges sniffing the world for seeing it.

It is interesting to note how two different breeds of dogs retrieve an object. A retriever will run after a thrown ball by marking its fall visually, chase in the general direction and look for it. A bloodhound will put his nose to the ground and blindly try to pick up a scent of the ball's bounce and follow its long roll. As von Uexküll[15] pointed out many years ago, the world of ours is and has been experienced quite differently by a tick, a snake, a fly, an urchin, a fish, or a bird. In the same respect, the world of humans is experienced differently by the Eskimo, the ecologist, the businessman, politician, or avant garde artist.

Benjamin Lee Whorf, a creative thinker in the field of linguistics, argues against the popular belief that human beings have a common logical structure that operates prior to and independently of communication through language. Whorf feels that the linguistic patterns themselves determine what the individual perceives in this world and how he thinks about it. He further hypothesizes that different linguistic systems result in different world views as in different awareness and action patterns or lifestyle attitudes. Thus, groups of people using differing linguistic patterns will think and perceive the world completely differently. Not all observers of the universe are led by the same physical evidence to the same picture of the universe. But groups of people having similar linguistic backgrounds will have similar universal views. In the words of Whorf:[16]

> We are thus introduced to a new principle of relativity which holds that all observers are not led by the same physical evidence to the same picture of the universe, unless their linguistic backgrounds are similar.... We cut up and organize the spread and flow of events as we do largely because, through our mother tongue, we are parties to an agreement to do so, not because nature itself is segmented in exactly that way for all to see.

A comparison of an Indo-European language group and an Indian language group illustrates how cultures using different linguistic structures have evolved. In Indo-European languages, subjects and verbs are basic grammatical units. Verbs have tenses which change according to the times spoken of and they also have active and passive voice. Thus it is possible to denote changes in time and voice as in the sentences: He kills. He killed. He will kill. He was killed. This emphasis on time and on active or passive behavior is very fundamental to a lot of western philosophy. Aristotle's categories of "substance," "attributes," and "action" and the antithesis of matter and force, mass and energy in physics are dependent on such underlying differentiations. Whorf[17] attributes the keeping of seconds, clocks, calendars, time used in physics, historical attitude, archaeology, etc., in Western culture to a linguistic emphasis on time. The Indian languages of Nootka (Vancouver Island) and Hopi, however, do not separate subjects and verbs or parts of speech. An event is signified as a whole. Nor does past, present, or future exist in Hopi. Whereas in English, we say, "a light flashed" or "it flashed," in Hopi one would simply say "flash." In Hopi, there is no difference among "he runs," "he is running," or "he ran." It is simply *wari* which is translated "running occur." The validity of a statement is determined not by tense but by fact, memory, custom or expectation. Therefore the future becomes an expectation and he will, shall, should or would is all *warinki* or translated "running occur, I dare say." Likewise then, a culture which does not emphasize time did not come up with the sophisticated instruments of chronology that Western cultures have. They live in timeless times.

In modern society, it is the artist who lives in other times. Through his art he represents the spirit of the future. It is through him – painter, sculptor, composer, filmmaker, dancer – and through his creations that man sees himself, his presence in the present, in the eyes of the future.

As Rainer Maria Rilke,[18] the German poet-philosopher, writes in his essay, "Ueber Kunst," "Again and again someone in the crowd wakes up, he has no ground in the crowd, and he emerges according to much broader laws. He carries strange customs with him and demands room for bold gestures. The future speaks ruthlessly through him." He further describes artists by saying that "Their winged heart everywhere beats against the walls of their time; their work was that which was not resolved in the lives they lived." This reminds me of Thoreau's[19] famous lines: "If a man does not keep pace with his companions, perhaps it is because he hears a different drummer. Let him step to the music he hears, however measured or far away."

And so it is that a personal attitude becomes a historical Zeitgeist which permeates not only an individual's outlook on life but the universal lifestyle attitude of an entire civilization. This attitude influences its language, its art, and its philosophy – in fact, every intellectual discipline. It is reflected in the varied use of the senses, in physiological patterns of the organism, in the structure of language, in man's relationship with his environment, etc. Biology, linguistics, the arts, ecology and the rest of the sciences – all are affected by personal and cultural attitudes. So, of course, is recreation. People who have been active in the recreation movement have much in common with avant-garde artists. They too, have been ahead of their times. Inspired by their heightened humanistic and ecological awareness, they have continued to emphasize the holistic character of man and his environment and the need for a recreative lifestyle attitude. I hope that soon the rest of the world will be able to hear their music and step to a different drummer.

15

A Panacea For Humanity

Perhaps the most powerful influence upon the lifestyle attitude of today's societies has been the emergence of modern science. The great discovery of the nineteenth century, according to Alfred North Whitehead, the British philosopher, was the discovery of the technique of discovery. Bertrand Russell carried this idea further by stating that the great discovery of the twentieth century was the technique of suspended judgment. In other words, you not only establish a direct relationship between cause and effect, but you also anticipate unwanted results and offset them before they actually happen. This "control of results" is the key to the scientific concept of determinism. It states that a given set of conditions leads to only one result. Consequently the one result obtained becomes a direct indication of whether or not a process under investigation is either right or wrong. Modern man incorporated this "either-or" method into all fields of human endeavor and began to look at the world strictly in terms of right or wrong, black or white, good or bad, etc. The Zeitgeist of determinsm was born.

The first statements of deterministic principles evolved in the seventeenth century. The three men who led the new scientific movement which marked the beginning of the Age of Reason were Kepler, who formulated laws that accurately described the motion of the planets; Galilei, who first introduced the idea of uniform acceleration and solved the problem of falling bodies; and Descartes, who postulated the concept *cogito ergo sum* (I think, therefore I am) and created the dualism of body and mind which is still haunting us today. The deterministic way of viewing the world in terms of direct cause-effect and either-or relationships became the basic premise of the Zeitgeist of modern man. From it developed a steadfast confidence in reason and science and the search for laws that governed life. This search eventually led to the application of scientific knowledge to practical problems. Science offered a certain truth and the practical application of this truth brought benefits to mankind. New insights and discoveries reduced ignorance and superstition and improved the quality of life. The human scene, in other words, profited from reason.

Deterministic principles began to permeate not only the sciences, but nearly all areas of life. In the field of medicine, for instance, fundamental contributions were made by such men as Robert Koch and Louis Pasteur. By establishing a direct cause-effect relationship between an illness and a microorganism, they originated the so-called germ theory of disease. Their work was completed by the development of countermeasures in the form of drugs and other treatment modalities to eradicate the germs and reestablish a condition of well-being. Man seemed to have found the way to health and the key to nature. These were the days of confidence and hope that eventually all natural processes would be explained and disease would be eliminated altogether. Toward the end of the eighteenth century, Laplace, a French astronomer and mathematician, stated the fundamental law of classical deterministic physics: *natura non facit saltus* (nature doesn't take leaps). He believed, in other words, that nature did not pull any surprises, but behaved in an ordered way, very much like a machine. Once enough knowledge of the underlying mechanistic principles of life on this earth is gained, man will achieve more and more control over his destiny. By becoming master over nature, there will be no limit to the improvement of the quality of human life. It was believed that the mechanistic world view of determinism would eventually provide answers for all world problems and serve as a panacea for humanity.

16

The Sorcerer's Apprentices

As time went by, modern man began to learn the hard way that nature doesn't operate like a machine. He also found out that a mechanistic approach to life has only limited possibilities and can become outright dangerous when followed exclusively. Perhaps the most disappointing fact was the realization that an increase in knowledge alone is not going to benefit mankind. Life, in other words, cannot be learned from a book. You need the wisdom of how to use the knowledge. Almost 200 years ago the German philosopher, Friedrich Schiller,[20] who was ten years younger than Laplace, was fully aware of the shortcomings of determinism when he wrote:

> . . . separated are pleasure from work, the means from the end, effect from satisfaction. Eternally confined to small fragments of the whole, man himself turns into fragment. Tuned into the monotonous grind of the wheel he never develops the harmony of himSELF and instead of integrating the humanity of his very nature he becomes a mere reflection of his business, his science . . . the dead word replaces the wisdom of living and a trained mind overpowers intuition and sensitivity.

Doesn't this sound as if it were written just yesterday? It sure does to me. What Schiller sensed 200 years ago is still very much with the world of today. Man still sees himself as master of nature. He interferes with the complexities of life in a variety of ways and develops a false feeling of precision and control. By thinking he is controlling nature, he automatically separates himself from it. But when you separate yourself from nature, you separate yourself from your own nature and lose touch with the wholeness of the universe.

This reminds me very much of Goethe's poem about the sorcerer's apprentice which describes very convincingly the dangers inherent in the mechanistic approach of determinism to life situations. I'm sure you remember Walt Disney's animated cartoon version complete with Mickey Mouse as the apprentice. It goes something like this: A famous sorcerer had to leave town and his apprentice could hardly wait to try out some of his master's tricks. So when he decided to take a bath, he remembered the sorcerer's words and made a broom carry up the water from the river to fill his bathtub. First he watched the scene with pride until suddenly he realized that he didn't know the right words to stop the broom. By that time the tub was overflowing and water began to pour down the stairs. In his desperation, he tried to kill the broom with an ax. But when he split the broom into two, to his bewilderment, two brooms were now running to fill the tub. Finally, the master returned, and said, *"Besen, Besen, sei's gewesen---"* and brought an end to this mess.

Unfortunately, mankind doesn't have a master to come to the rescue. It gets stuck with the mess it creates. The calamity with DDT[21] illustrates this dilemma well. It was a proud occasion when the quality of life was improved by eliminating mosquitoes with DDT spray. At last people could enjoy summer evenings outside without being eaten alive by insect pests. But the feeling of pride didn't last very long. Soon it was found out that DDT not only killed the insects, but also was absorbed by the human body and poisoned it. Particularly fearful was the fact that these toxic substances can be passed on from a pregnant woman to her fetus. And then to further compound the situation, some strains of mosquitoes evolved which were able to resist the insecticide. The same is true of antibiotics, the so-called miracle drugs. Due to overprescription, strains of bacteria, unaffected by penicillin and such, are evolving. The "technique of suspended judgment," as Bertrand Russell called it, certainly has its shortcomings and simply doesn't always work. I am sure you can add your own examples of pollution caused by both products and waste products of our technology. Not only are people directly affected by them, but our shortsighted technological progress has cast its ugly shadow on rivers, forests, oceans, and the air.

Speaking of the air, one of the major contributors to air pollution is, of course, the automobile. But what has been done about this problem during the past fifty years? Not much, as I see it. On the contrary, the big car companies have basically produced the same old cars for decades. Where was the research? Where were the plans for developing significant alternatives for the gas guzzling and air polluting gasoline engines? All they have done is retool for changes in the styling of their new models. It seems obvious that the big car companies are interested only in profit and ignore the fact that they have a responsibility toward society. With this type of leadership coming from major industries, what does the future hold? If the country continues to support these priorities you might one day have to buy yourself a gas mask and learn to live side-by-side with the increased air pollution. Quite conceivably, it might be possible to order one out of the Sears catalog, in decorator colors to match your shirt, your shoes, your handbag, and your acid rain umbrella. The public might also be told that the country can't afford to eliminate the air pollution caused by cars because too many people are working in the gas mask industry. They will have to stay employed to guarantee a "healthy" economy. I am not kidding when I say this. Some of these things are already with us today.

To speak of the health of the economy and in terms of cost and profit in reference to critical issues affecting life on this planet is outright insane. Too many people apparently still can't grasp the fact that it is not money that supports the ecosystem and all the living creatures in it, but the earth, the water, and the air. Their lifestyle attitude is dangerously polluted by outdated merchant values. If you add the worldwide political immaturity to all of this, you can't help but wonder where all this lunacy is leading. I don't dare think about nuclear proliferation, laser weapons, genetic engineering, arsenals in space, and all those scary things people are experimenting with in all corners of the globe. Aren't all those

53

known disasters from the past enough to teach the world a lesson? How many more atomic explosions, acid rain phenomena, pesticide poisonings, Three Mile Island incidents and Love Canals will it take to wake people up.

The natural environment is mankind's most precious possession and the most basic factor determining the quality of life for generations to come. The recreation movement is in the forefront of helping people raise their consciousness regarding their attitude toward the environment and the realization that they are a part of it all. Recreation will continue its role as a vanguard in the protection of our natural resources and its fight against all those sorcerer's apprentices who threaten our very existence with their ignorance, greed and irresponsibility.

17

Experts and Labels are Suspect

Yes, determinism is alive and well today. In the field of medicine, it is referred to by its opponents as the "overestablishment of the doctrine of specificity."[22] Not much has changed since the days of Koch and Pasteur. The cause-effect approach is still very much the standard treatment procedure and illness is dealt with in very specific terms. Medicine is basically still looking at disease as the result of something interfering with healthy life. It then directs all of its efforts toward finding this "something" and looking for a way to eliminate it. The sequence of effect, cause, and countermeasure is known as the *classical treatment model* which still dominates the field of medicine and all related helping professions. However, I am not discrediting this approach altogether. If, for instance, you happen to have a growth on your liver, you'd better find somebody who knows how to get to your liver and cut out the growth without killing you. He should be able to very deterministically follow the necessary procedures. In a case like this, the classical treatment approach is expedient, beneficial, and in all respects well justified.

But what concerns me is the fact that this deterministic treatment approach is carried too far and often into areas where its application is out of place or even downright dangerous. I am referring particularly to the social sciences and all the diseases and problems of living which cannot be traced to a specific cause. In spite of the extremely limited knowledge about certain disorders, symptoms are described, characteristics analyzed, and finally the subject under investigation is labeled with long impressive names and treated accordingly. Alice Morgan is a schizophrenic. What is covered up by this term is the fact that nobody really knows what the disease is that they are describing. When it comes right down to it, schizophrenia is a concept only. In books which catalog various disorders with long detailed descriptions of symptoms and behavior patterns, only in small print and at the very end of the writeup does it state that the disease is "of unknown etiology" or "idiopathic." In plain English that means that nothing is known about the cause of it. Still, and this is very frightening, the so-called "experts" deal with these labels as if they were established realities and intervene with very specific treatment modalities as if they knew what they were doing.

A perfect example of the power of labels is a book of labels used by people in the helping professions, from chief psychiatrists to health insurance agents. It is called *Diagnostic and Statistical Manual of Mental Disorders*,[23] 3rd edition, or DSM-III for short. Listed and described in it are commonly known forms of mental illness. A relatively small percentage or disorders have pretty well established causes such as brain damage, alcoholism, or drug abuse. The vast majority, however, are disorders categorized and labeled rather subjectively on the basis of preconceived criteria. The labels resulting from this procedure have become so real to experts and laity alike that they are accepted as the absolute truth. They don't realize that there are many other ways of looking at these problems of living which could produce entirely different sets of labels. As a matter of fact, even labels such as disorder, disease, and illness are questionable in this context. Let me illustrate to you how many of these categories and special words have originated.

Pretend that you want to find some curtains for a room in your house. You go to a fabric store and look around. It takes a while to orient yourself and figure out that the textiles are arranged according to the material, i.e., silk, wool, rayon, polyester, etc. You can't seem to find what you want, so you drive to another store. You immediately try the "material model" from the last store but, to your surprise, the saleslady at this store has the fabrics arranged by color. They are laid out in the order of the rainbow. You again can't find what you want, and so you visit another store. After you try to locate your fabric according to material and then by color, based on your past experiences, you discover a new, sophisticated system. Here the textiles are rated on a scale based on their acoustic qualities, from materials that reflect sound rather harshly to the ones which absorb it softly. Completely baffled, you try one more store and find the curtain materials labeled according to function: curtains for the bedroom, bath, the children's room, the den, garage or kitchen. They even have an elaborate questionnaire designed by a psychologist who coordinates color with function. After filling out the questionnaire, you discover the reasons for your unsatisfactory sex life: you have the wrong curtains in your bedroom. Sounds outrageous? The fact is, a leading German textile company waged a four-year advertising campaign in the early seventies promoting psychologically sound drapery selections. The point I want to make is that you have to be very careful in the way you use certain words and in the way you accept systems of labeling. Systems are built on preconceived concepts, and words within a system are most of the time limited to it. Outside of the system, the word may mean nothing or may limit the real thing is describes. The old adage, "You tell a child the name of a bird and he doesn't see the bird anymore" is a good example of this phenomenon. Dr. Albert Einstein[24] expressed a similar idea when he wrote in memoriam to Dr. Ernst Mach, a Viennese physicist:

> Concepts which have proved useful for ordering things easily assume so great an authority over us, that we forget their terrestrial origin and accept them as unalterable facts. They then become labeled as "conceptual" necessities. The road of scientific progress is frequently blocked for long periods by such errors.

What holds true for scientific progress is even more applicable to the sphere of human living. There, more than anywhere else, experts and labels are suspect.

18

The Champion of the Underdog

Labels are not only suspect but often downright dangerous. The IQ label which has long been cherished as a tool for measuring intelligence has finally been attacked as a biased and subjective analysis. Minority groups, who long suffered with inferior labeling from culturally biased instruments, have taken issue with the IQ test. Schools no longer use IQ tests as exclusive indicators of retardation or giftedness. Even the armed services have discarded mass use of IQ tests. It is now considered to be a partial indicator of aptitude to be used with caution. Human beings vary in their ability to perform in a test situation. There are good test takers and bad test takers. Furthermore, the IQ test itself doesn't begin to measure such aspects of "intelligence" as creativity, sense of humor, musical, artistic and athletic talents, etc. And it must not be forgotten that generations of mislabeled persons have been shuffled through mentally handicapped classrooms, through stunted military careers, and psychiatric institutions – all because of mislabeling.

Recreators don't deal with people on the basis of labels, disorders, or disabilities. For them, such nomenclature is of only secondary importance. In this way, interacting with people in a recreational setting differs completely from the classical treatment model. The recreator relates to the person as another human being as if nothing would be wrong with him. This does not mean that he ignores the fact that his client has a certain handicap or label, but he doesn't let it enter into the actual relationship. The recreator and the client establish a human bond which becomes the core of their interaction. The label, at best, serves as background information only.

Recreators are not interested in changing or treating people. They realize people have to do this themselves. Their participation has to be self-appropriated. They must be intrinsically motivated. In this sense, the individual is his own expert. He alone decides his limitations, aspirations and how, when and where he wants to participate. The recreator takes nothing for granted, but facilitates the process of recreation by serving the individual in his recreative pursuits. Therein lies his expertise.

It is, for example, a well-known fact that one of the greatest problems of being blind is the social stigma of *blindism*. It has nothing to do with the person nor with being blind. All it is is the preconceived idea of so-called experts, who tell everybody of how a blind person should be treated. You should do this or you shouldn't do that with them. The victims of this type of "knowledge," of course, have been the blind. Many young people who don't have their eyesight have been overprotected and restricted. They have had only limited opportunities to develop special skills and to rid themselves of excess energy. As a result, many blind people develop random movements and related psychological problems.

In contrast, I have been personally involved in conducting ski programs for amputees, blind individuals, people over seventy, and for youths with various birth defects. None of those labels kept them from learning to ski as a recreative experience. For me they were Fred, Mary, Sue, and John, the skiers. They told me what they could or couldn't do and together we found solutions to their problems. In recreation it is the personal relationship and the milieu that count. Labels are unimportant and the individual is his own expert. The relationship might be diagrammed like this:

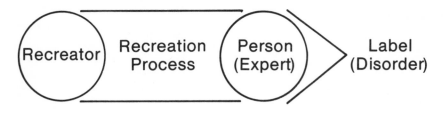

In a classical treatment model, a therapist concentrates on the label and relates to it in terms of treatment. The client as a person is of only limited significance. The label and the treatment process are the center of attention. It can be diagrammed like this:

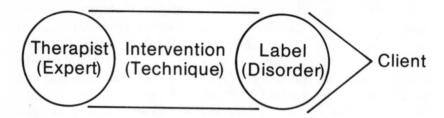

Many human beings who have had the *wrong* labels attached to them have ended up on the periphery of everyday living. I am thinking of handicapped, culturally deprived, racially discriminated against and emotionally disturbed individuals, of older adults, and of all those lumped together under the questionable label of *special populations*. Recreation throughout the years has been an ideal and proven process in assisting these people to find their way into the mainstream of life. Recreation is the champion of the underdog!

19

Experience Precedes Experiment

Determinism, with its labels and quick answers for everything, is all around us and still dominates our lifestyle. It has infiltrated all areas of modern living from technology to education, and from working with computers to living with people. As I have pointed out before, it has done a lot of good in improving the quality of life on this planet but it also has done and is still doing a lot of damage to the world. Is there anything to help us curb such negative influences? I think so. It is the shift from a strictly mechanistic to a holistic Zeitgeist that operates under *indeterministic* principles.

In contrast to deterministic principles, in which a given set of conditions leads to one result only, indeterministic principles include the observer in the experiment. The way the observer sets up the hypothesis determines the result. He cannot escape his own experience. A given set of conditions, therefore, can lead to two or more results depending on how many hypotheses have been introduced. In other words, the experience of the observer influences the outcome of the experiment.

This world view has been with us for a long time. As far back as the thirteenth century, Roger Bacon[25] pointed out the importance of experience. He is considered to be the grandfather of modern science and is the first one ever to use the phrase *experimental science* in Part VI of his *Opus Majus*. He wrote:

> I now wish to unfold the principles of experimental science, since without experience nothing can be sufficiently known. For there are two modes of acquiring knowledge, namely, by *reasoning* and *experience*. Reasoning draws a conclusion and makes us grant the conclusion, but does not make the conclusion certain, nor does it remove doubt so that the mind may rest on the intuition of truth, unless the mind discovers it by the path of experience.

Bacon is said to have learned the difference between "reasoning" and "knowing through actual experience" from Saracen sources. The inductive process of the scientific method which we developed in the Western world has its origin in this doctrine. Modern science, however, instead of incorporating the necessity "to experience" into all realms of man's life, limited the meaning of the Latin word *"experior"* to "to experiment" only. It thereby removed the human dimension, the consciousness of the experimenter, from the experiment. From then on, Western science approached the acquisition of knowledge by *experiment* only and no longer by means of itself, that is, by *experience*.

On December 14, 1900, when Max Planck announced for the first time his "Quantum Theory," he laid the foundation for an indeterministic Zeitgeist that brought experience back into the experiment. He revised the deterministic doctrine which states that nature does not take any leaps by asking if nature did anything else *but take* leaps. With that, the classical, deterministic period of physics came to an end. By 1930, indeterministic principles were pretty well established and began to infiltrate not only the sciences but other areas of human endeavor. They were originally developed from the Second Law of Thermodynamics and dealt with the exploration of the true nature of light. The result of this exploration was the fact that light behaved either like particles or like waves, depending on the type of observation applied. Neither description excludes the other and each must be supported by special properties to give it meaning. In other words, how you look at light will determine what you are going to get. If you set up your hypothesis one way, you end up with a wave-model and if you set it up another way, you end up with a particle-model. Your experience is *in* the experiment; "how you see is what you get!" as I pointed out before.

In 1927 Heisenberg[26] announced the "Principle of Indeterminacy or Uncertainty" for the first time. It asserts that limitations inherent in nature prohibit the determination of both the position and the velocity of a particle. The future course of a particle cannot be predicted unless both velocity and position at a given moment are known. Most scientists since have agreed that causality is indeterminable and must be abandoned as a scientific concept. The principle of indeterminacy, as I mentioned before, holds that a given set of conditions can lead to more than one result depending on the nature of the observation. The different results do not cancel each other out, but are all accepted on an equal basis. The wave-model and the particle-model exist side by side and complement each other. Bohr[27] developed from this concept the "Principle of Complementarity" which states that mutual exclusiveness changes into coexistence.

Let me give you a practical analogy. Imagine five preschool children sitting on the floor in a circle and holding hands while a group of adults looks on. The teacher says, "Please stretch out your legs and reach inward with your arms. Pretend you all are a giant flower. Each of you represents one beautiful petal of it. What do flowers do during the night? They close up; they sleep. You are closed up; you are sleeping. Now the morning has arrived, the sun rises above the horizon and the outer petals start to unfold. Slowly raise your arms until you are all stretched out on the floor. Now the sun is almost straight above you and the inner petals begin to open up. Lift your legs, higher and higher, and slowly lower them over your head until your toes touch the floor. Now the sun is on its way down and you slowly, slowly return to your original position." The children's bodies move in unison with the instructions and in childlike fashion, their imaginations soar.

What does this exercise have to do with the principles of quantum theory? The children imagined they were flower petals. They experienced themselves as all kinds of flowers in a variety of colors. Each child developed from the same exercise his very own, specific "flower model." The kindergarten teacher who watched what was going on said to herself, "What a nice way to give children the opportunity to act out their fantasies." She ended up with a "fantasy model." A gentleman, who thinks of himself as a peda-gogue, noticed that the authority shifted from the leader to the group. And Johnny, who usually acts up, was kept in place by the other four kids in the group. You could say he conceptualized a "shift of authority model." The physiologist in the crowd saw the exercise as a fun way of introducing stomach muscle strengthen-ing exercises to children. His turned out to be a "fitness model." Each child and each of the three adults looked at the exercise through a different pair of glasses, so to speak. The glasses, of course, represent their own frame of reference, their personal Zeitgeist. They got what they saw. The models they arrived at individually, complement each other and collectively enrich the insight into the exercise. Still, the door is open for further possibilities, for other models.

Recreation operates under indeterministic principles. Experi-ence precedes experiment.

20

Happiness Comes Incidentally

Indeterminism helps us to understand that life is an open-ended process. It constantly creates new expressions and remains open for them. It is accident-prone. Living organisms are not closed systems; they are not machines. By transferring the indeterministic principles of physics into the field of biology, Bohr united the exact sciences with the life sciences and is therefore considered the father of the modern unity of sciences. Macrophysics, which concerns itself with explorations of outer space, has also joined the ranks of indeterminism. I am sure most of you have heard about the theories of curved space and black holes. Scientists think that these invisible non-objects may help explain the universe. The theories surrounding them are all open-ended. They do not allow for a definite prediction of the position or the velocity of a particle or any combination of the two. All that can be predicted is the probability that certain particles will be emitted. As you can see, vagueness is inherent to modern physics. And to make things ever more vague, Professor Ornstein[28] from Stanford seriously questions the mathematical soundness of probability. In his monograph he constructed an example of indeterministic processes that cannot be modeled by traditional probabilistic structures. He insists that it is simply *not* true that all indeterministic processes arise from "roulette-type" mechanisms. You can see that the rejection of determinism as an explanation of natural events has an impact not only on our understanding of life but also on the nature of random processes. We have come a long way since Einstein's famous quotation: "God does not play dice." The propositions of contemporary science suggest that God is indeed playing dice and to make things even more difficult for us, he throws them sometimes where we can't see them.[29]

The open-ended model with its emphasis on process rather than on goal orientation is by now a well-accepted concept within the epistemology of contemporary science. Interestingly enough, among disciplines much "softer" than the hard science of physics, the *Kausalitätsbedürfnis* (the need for immediate causality), is still most prevalent. This observation is particularly true of the social sciences and of certain areas in the field of medicine where highly complex aspects of living continue to be approached with deterministic methodologies. The classical sequence of "headache – take Aspirin – no more headache" still prevails as the prominent treatment approach for the helping professions.

Recreation doesn't work that way. Recreators accept the fact that there are no straight answers or pills against depression or loneliness, just as there are none for spontaneity or sociability. You can't drug people into happiness, nor can you coerce them to be creative or to fall in love. What you can do is establish a milieu conducive to the discovery and the development of these characteristics. The process of recreation provides such a milieu. But, there is no specific way, nor is there a guarantee of reaching these preconceived goals. On the contrary, most of the time nothing can keep a person further away from them than a direct pursuit. Nathaniel Hawthorne wrote in the mid-nineteenth century:

Happiness in this world, when it comes,
comes incidentally.
Make it the object of pursuit, and it leads
us on a wild goose chase, and is never attained.
Follow some other object, and very possibly we
may find we have caught happiness without dreaming of it.

When you have a recreative lifestyle attitude, you are in pursuit of nonpursuit. That doesn't mean that the process of recreation is totally without pursuit or without goals. It means only that the setting of goals is limited to processes that lend themselves to a deterministic approach. The learning and improvement of skills is an excellent example. Hopefully the new skill levels will indirectly lead to the acquisition of characteristics such as increased joy, self-confidence, sociability and a recreative lifestyle attitude. "Open-ended" then means that nobody knows in advance what the final outcome of the entire recreation process is going to be since changes arise from moment to moment and from situation to situation. Even if goals are restricted to the acquisition and improvement of specific skills, the same program plan, in spite of being followed religiously, will have different results with different people. Experienced recreators who realize this will intuitively respond with adjustments in the program plan as the recreative process is evolving. It is this provision of and readiness for spontaneous and creative change which give recreation its unique appeal and strength. Attitudes of inner peace, of camaraderie, of trust or of happiness cannot be pursued directly as final goals. They merely arise from situations that are conducive to the discovery and emergence of such attitudes. A truly recreative milieu provides such situations and has its origins in the lifestyle attitude of people who are at leisure. Recreation is an open-ended process. Happiness comes incidentally.

21

Responding To Yourself

The concept of process orientation and the open-ended model are rarely understood by other professionals who work side by side with recreators. The need for objectives, goals, and evaluations in their own specialties is so great that they have difficulty accepting anyone who does not operate under the same principles. All they can see is that the recreator "throws out the ball." What they can't see, for instance, is that during the ball game, Mr. Smith got off his chair for the first time in weeks. Was this planned? Of course it wasn't planned; it just happened like so many other things that happen within the complex realms of recreational settings. What is even more difficult for them to accept is the fact that the best way to have kept Mr. Smith on his chair would have been to plan to get him off it. They are so conditioned to the need of having full control over a situation that an approach of "letting it be" or "doing nothing" is out of their comprehension. This reminds me of what the great British actor, Sir Alec Guinness[30] had to say about his acting when he accepted a special Oscar for his contributions to the film industry. In his words:

> . . . You know, when I was a drama student, 47 years ago I think, there used to be a formidable lady who came to give

classes of what she called "Film Technique" and she arrived with a large wooden frame about four foot square which she placed in front of our faces saying it was a closeup and then she barked at us, "Show fear, anger, joy, despair" — and I quickly learned how to get maybe a laugh or two out of my fellow students; and then it dawned on me that if I was seriously going to have a career in movies the wisest thing was *to do absolutely nothing at all;* and that is more or less what I've done since then.[32]

For most people, being scientific still means to be deterministic, to have a goal, to systematically go after it, and eventually come up with one result. I tell you in all honesty I have done my best work as a psychotherapist when *I* was secure enough to do nothing. It is the ideal role of a facilitator to initiate a process and then to allow the process to take over. Do you know how difficult this is to do? When you accept a dollar a minute, you feel you absolutely must do something. You think that you at least should make your client cry or scream by trying out this technique or by following that theory. The need to satisfy one's own insecurities, pride, or sense of duty by *treating* another person is overpowering. To treat, by the way, comes from the Latin word *"tractare"* which means "to pull." Most people who work with people unfortunately are pullers or manipulators. Recreators don't treat, nor do they manipulate. They facilitate. They realize that even if you have the most sincere desire to help a person, that person still can make you a part of his plan to destroy himself and there is not a thing you can do about it. It also works the other way around. There are those working with people who are so enamored by their program, their techique, or their personal need to treat that they forget they are dealing with human beings. It was Thoreau who once said, "If I knew that a man was coming to my house with the conscious design of doing me good, I should run for my life." Recreators are therapists in the true sense of the word. Therapy comes from the Greek word *therapeutin* which means "to serve." People in recreation are servants to their clients. They serve by providing a milieu that is conducive to helping their clients to assume responsibility. What is responsibility? Responsibility is the ability to respond. To whom? To themselves. The process of recreation provides an ideal training ground to practice responding to one's SELF in a nonthreatening milieu out of which spontaneity, joy, friendship, relaxation and, above all, a recreative lifestyle attitude can evolve. The process of recreation is based upon the acceptance of the theoretical constructs of indeterminancy and complementarity. Recreators operate under principles of contemporary science, and the process of recreation provides abundant opportunities for responding to yourself.

22

To Be Or Not To Be At Leisure

The message received from the Zeitgeist of contemporary science is very clear. The direct cause-effect model of determinism has outlived its usefulness in the exploration of nature. Mechanistic principles are to be applied under well-defined and limited circumstances only. As such, they will continue to serve man in his striving to improve the quality of life. If, on the other hand, man continues to ignore the far-reaching importance of indeterminism in his dealings with the complexities of nature and human living, he will be paving the way for his own downfall. As Lewis Thomas[31] wrote in his essay "On Science and Uncertainty,"

> We are nowhere near completion. The greatest achievements in the science of this century are themselves the source of more puzzlement than human beings have ever experienced. Indeed, it is likely that the twentieth century will be looked back at as the time when science provided the first close glimpse of the profundity of human ignorance. We have not reached solutions; we have only begun to discover how to ask questions.

Science is not static; it is a dynamic concept. Experiment and experience have been united into a principle of complementarity.

71

Out of this development, science has gained much more than a new method. It has been enriched beyond strictly quantitative valuations by allowing qualitative information in the description of life. In an experiment, you are objectively detached and only intellectually connected. In an experience, if you want to be or not, you are subjectively involved and intuitively connected. You have a naive awareness of yourself and everything around you. Ludwig von Bertalanffy[32] observed that ". . .in quantum physics, the object of research is not nature itself anymore, but man's investigation of nature. At the end of physical research, man confronts himself alone."

This subjective connection of man and his science, hopefully, will lead not only to a unification of the sciences but provide man with the type of scientific morality which is so much needed in the world today. The experience of life is available to anyone. So-called "experts" become highly suspect. They tend to oversimplify the sensitive and complex phenomena of life and living. Their insistence that they are dealing with life on a strictly objective basis gives them a false sense of security, precision, and control. They deny any subjective involvement and value judgment. It is for this reason that modern man is in need of a scientific method that provides an understanding of nature and of his own nature with as few abstractions as possible. "The knower has to be caught in the act of paying attention to what is happening in him, to him, and around him.[33] By changing from a mechanistic to a holistic Zeitgeist, the key question no longer is "What shall I know?" but "How shall I live?"

People have been led to believe that advanced technology, better physicians, new drugs, larger hospitals and, above all, more research will improve the quality of life on this earth. I am convinced that in the long run none of these will. The major breakthrough will have to come from the individual—from you. How? By returning the responsibility for your own health and well-being to you. You have to decide how you want to live and then—and this is the difficult part—actually live that way. "To be or not to be at leisure"—that is the question.

PART II

PLAYING AT LIFE

23

Working At Leisure

What you don't understand, you can't make your own. Leisure is impossible if people don't know what it is. During the past twenty years, society has dramatically increased its understanding of such notions as ecology, handicaps, and nutrition. The average person can at least pay lip service to environmental issues even if it's only an annual trip to the recycling center. He is aware of some basic needs and programs for the handicapped even it it's only a reserved parking space in the supermarket lot. And he attends to new nutritional guidelines even if it's only passing up the salt shaker at dinner time. But as for a basic understanding of the concept of leisure, the average man still functions in the Dark Ages. The modern masses still misconstrue leisure as anything from "free time" to "partying" to even "laziness." At the extreme, it is even equated with drugs as in the popular phrase "recreational drug use" or sexual acrobatics as evident in the barrage of books, videos and films on the subject. To understand what has led to the modern misuse of the concept of leisure, let's briefly trace its evolution from ancient times to the present.

The word, leisure, has its origin in the Greek word, *skole*. *Skole* means to halt, to hold back, or to ease off — easing off in the sense of ceasing any form of distress or ceasing the obligation to labor. It means to have quiet or inner peace, or to have the time and condition for cultivating the *self*. When a person is at ease, when he has inner peace, he is at leisure. From the Greek *skole* also comes the English word "school" or "scholarship." Interestingly, this connects leisure with the free disposal of time to pursue education, not only in the sense of learning, but in the development of culture and enlightenment.

The Latin base for the term leisure is the word, *licere*, which means to be permitted. From this word comes the English word "license" meaning permission, permission to do as one pleases, or to be as one pleases.

The early Greek philosopher, Aristotle,[1] dealt with the concept of leisure in his famous *Politics*. In it, he ties leisure directly to contemplation, the condition in which man has time to think or ponder and do for himself what he chooses. In opposition to leisure, Aristotle speaks of war in which "the cause" does not allow the individual to contemplate. He notes that the Spartans misused their leisure which was the result of periods of peace. Therefore, they did not experience leisure in the pure sense, but only as spare time or the time between wars. The Spartans were only effective as long as they were engaged in war which for them was work. Once there was no more war, life ceased to be meaningful and their state deteriorated. Even the Spartan women, when given time galore, used it for license, not for leisure. They became corrupt and were unable to be at peace during peace times. The Spartans just couldn't handle leisure.

For Aristotle, leisure was the freedom from toil and a state of existence in which everything is done for its own sake or as an end in itself. It was an ideal to be sought. This early concept of leisure is not time based at all. It is *attitude* based. It is not spare time or free time or vacation time or comp time because periods of existence based on time can be misused attitudinally. Leisure in the true Greek sense of the word is a lifestyle attitude in which the person is free from the necessity of being occupied. Leisure is a state of being in which activity, if any, is an end in itself.

The ancient Greeks chose music and contemplation as the two main pursuits of leisure. Whether alone or in the pleasure of good company, they enjoyed music performed by minstrels and playing music themselves, and they reveled in the opportunity to discuss, to ponder, and to contemplate. Through music and contemplation, they sought to achieve the wholeness and peacefulness and oneness with life, as men doing what they chose for its own sake.

Needless to say, the Greeks were supported by a system of slavery which allowed the privileged class to achieve leisure at the expense of the masses.

Later, the Romans also considered the ideal of leisure, but more as the opposite of nonleisure. The Latin word *otium*, the leisure state, was considered only in relationship to its opposite, *negotium*, the nonleisure or business state. Therefore, leisure was not conceived for its own sake, but only as a contrast to the state of nonleisure which was business or "busy-ness," as the word was originally written.

A Roman who was tired from the demands of *negotium* would then pursue *otium* as a replenishment. According to Roman thought, the well-spent life was centered on *negotium* which carried the most worth or importance. The Roman busily attacked the problems of daily living, of government, business, trade, etc., and then he rested from them.

It is in the Roman culture that we see the beginnings of the contemporary work ethic. Empire building, business, law, and bureaucracy were major contributions to the world by the Roman culture and, as such, necessitated hard work and diligent perseverance. The infamous ruler, Cato the Elder, applauded hard work, speaking to the farmers, "Do not lie around, but clean up, for cessation of work is not accompanied by cessation of expenses."[2]

The Roman philosopher, Seneca, expanded the idea of leisure when he insisted that everyone needs leisure "for only in the state of leisure can a man choose the model by which to direct his life."[3] In this respect, the leisured life is a philosophical state, even if the Roman conception of leisure was primarily a rest from work.

The Christian concept of leisure has a similarity to both the Greek idea of contemplation and the Roman dualistic concept of toil versus amusement. But the essential difference between the Greek concept of leisure and the Christian is that contemplation is no longer seen as an end in itself, but as a divine pursuit. The Christian contemplates God and in so doing seeks Divine Truth. The end becomes more important than the act itself. It is more important to seek God, to save one's soul and to pursue the afterlife than to seek oneself, one's relationship to life and contemplate the earthly life. Thomas Aquinas, the great religious thinker, maintained that contemplation of God brings about perfect happiness.

With the collapse of the Roman Empire, the world was once

again plunged into a fight for survival and the need for manual labor was crucial. Therefore, to the early Christians, work was a virtue and idleness a vice. In the words of Saint Benedict, "Idleness is the enemy of the soul."[4] Whereas early Christianity still contemplated to understand the Creator and His universe, late medieval Christians contemplated in order to figure out nature and change it to suit man's needs.

The Age of Reason brought the idea that man was the center of the universe and the keys to the universe were discoverable through scientific means. Nature could be subdued, controlled and transformed to suit man. By this control or transformation came the re-emphasis of the dignity of work. The major difference between ancient times in which leisure rescued man from toil, and the post-Renaissance in which work was reasonably glorified, was the type of labor given dignity. Men of the post-Renaissance dignified nonagrarian manual labor in the form of crafts, sciences, and arts, all of which were pursued during his "free time" if not his leisure. And still, the masses labored on so the privileged could have leisure. The concept of leisure had become corrupted as a means to an end. Leisure was not an end in itself to complete man or nourish the inner self, but rather a means to unlock the universal secrets and harness the world.

As the eighteenth century emerged, the glorification of the work act was fully realized. Adam Smith's[5] famous *The Wealth of Nations* associated the task of turning raw materials into useful articles as a truly productive act. The workers and the act of working was seen as productive, honorable and admirable. The work ethic had arrived. With the industrial society and its accompanying technology, work flourished as laborers united with machines to produce and to profit. Work was considered the passage to wealth.

With the coming of the twentieth century, the work ethic reigned. Capitalists, Communists, and fascists, Christians, Moslems and Jews—a varied assortment of groups and creeds all subscribed to one common idea, the goodness of hard labor.

And so the Greek ideal of leisure as a state of being, as an attitude, as an end in and of itself disappeared. As civilization advanced through the Protestant Reformation, the Age of Reason, and the Industrial Revolution, leisure came to mean an assortment of things like absence from work, free time, idleness, amusement, rest, and even sin.

In the postindustrial society of the twentieth century, the concept has gone through a further philosophical change. Consumerism has become a way of life for the growing middle and upper classes. With the lust to consume, to buy, and to collect comes the need to work and acquire more money in order to purchase more things. Second jobs, women's jobs, adolescent's jobs are commonplace. Coexisting with the need to work is the need for leisure, but the major emphasis is not on a state of being or an attitude, but rather on relaxation, amusement, and distraction.

Modern twentieth century societies recognize man's need to relax and to be amused or diverted from the daily humdrum of work. Parks and recreational facilities abound, and an assortment of organized programs and diversional activities are eagerly pursued. The underlying difference between the original Greek ideal and the mid-twentieth century concept of leisure is that modern man pursues leisure the same way he pursues work. His lifestyle attitude has not changed, and the original Greek ideal has been lost. Modern man works at leisure.

24

Values Rooted in Travail

As we have seen in ancient Greece, leisure was not bound to time, nor was it tied to work. Leisure was an ideal, timeless and free from utility. It was the total freedom from the necessities of toil and exertion, and it intrinsically contained pleasure, happiness and the joy of life. It was, in fact, the very essence of life. If they could have heard the slogan "the right to work" and observed all the glorifications of work that industrialized man has concocted, they would have been astounded. How then did the glorification of labor begin? And how did this viewpoint become so firmly entrenched in contemporary society?

Throughout the ages and until quite recently, the human condition was dominated by scarcity. It took a lot of energy to produce enough to guarantee man's survival. And the major source of energy was human muscle power. In addition, man also learned to use the muscle power of animals, to employ fire and later to harness water and wind with relatively simple tools. All this energy and labor were necessary in order to exist.

Then came the great transition from a rather stable agricultural society to an industrial one, or the shifting from a tool age to a machine age. In history this whole era is referred to as the Industrial Revolution, which was not a sudden development, but really a gradual one. Man created a vast repertoire of energy sources: coal, steam, gasoline, elecricity, solar, thermal, tidal and nuclear energies, to name a few.

Wassily Leontief,[6] a Nobel Prize winner in economics, analyzed the development of the industrial society. He points out that with a marked increase in productivity, the capacity to consume lags more and more behind. Leontief maintains that until the Great Depression, productivity and consumption were pretty well balanced. Then, for the first time, consumption caught up with productivity and suddenly there was less need for human energy to produce. The direct implication of this increased productivity was the diminished need for human labor. And this trend, from thereon, has been well demonstrated in the increase of unemployment in all industrialized nations.

Several years ago, the economist, G. F. Hanke,[7] predicted growing unemployment based on the principle of productivity exceeding consumption, a direct result of advancing technology. He concluded that in order to balance this new relationship between productivity and consumption, working time must be shortened. To a certain extent, this has already taken place. But the decrease in working time has only been hailed as a social improvement, not as a means to balance productivity with consumption. Whereas adults and children used to work twelve hours a day, seven days a week, the new society works eight hours a day, five days a week, and child labor laws prohibit children from working. Ironically, though, as work time lessened and conditions improved, the work act was made even more desirable. In capitalistic countries, work was glorified for profit. In communistic countries, it was deemed a contribution to the state, and in religious teaching, it was hailed for the purification of the soul or the escape from idleness.

So instead of striving for leisure, as in the Greek society, we have a striving for work. Indeed, work has become the central force of the ethical structure of society. Generations of Americans have been raised with such phrases as "Idleness is the Devil's workshop" or "Idle hands make idle minds" which stress the importance of "busy-ness." Readers like the famous *New England Primer* and other more recent textbooks have long espoused the virtues of work. In Hitler's Germany, the Nazis used to say *"Arbeit macht frei"* (Work makes free), and present-day socialist countries likewise have similar slogans. The Soviet flag brandishes the hammer and sickle, symbols of the industrial and agricultural worker.

Most admittedly, the work ethic had a purpose during the progress of civilization, first in the name of sheer survival and then for materialistic gains. Perhaps even "dissonance reduction" caused man to accept and glorify that which was necessary and could not be avoided.

The problem in the twentieth century is that the work ethic ceases to have purpose as automation and technology replace manual labor. Productivity now exceeds consumption and unemployment rages. Still the political cry is "Put every man back to work!" With such shortsightedness does twentieth century man operate, from the political policymaker to the unemployed man in the street. Very few industrial countries have undertaken to shorten the work week in order to absorb more people into the shrinking job market.

Now that we suddenly have too many goods and not enough scarcity, the labor problem becomes paramount. The idea of shortening the work week to counteract increased productivity has again surfaced but for a different reason, this time not to improve working conditions, but to counterbalance the threat of overproduction. As Hanke points out, this reduction in total work hours must not in any way reduce the purchasing power, nor should it have any impact on the cost of the product. And this view presents a very difficult problem for modern man to resolve: to pay the same wages for less work and yet maintain the same purchasing power. In simple words it would mean that people would have more time. They would work less, produce less, but products would still cost the same and people would make the same wages. Under this system, the working conditions and the work ethic would have to undergo very basic changes. More meaning would have to be found in the work process itself and extended into the additional free time made available. This is the challenge of leisure. If this challenge is not met, and if the existing practices and values of our society are rigidly maintained, the consequences will be disastrous.

Unfortunately, they still are being rigidly maintained by nearly all levels of modern society, by teachers, preachers, parents, and peers, from popular newspaper columnists whose "advice" is ingested by the masses to leaders in business and politics.

I remember a recent column of "Ask Ann Landers"[8] in which a worried writer objected that the Protestant work ethic was fast becoming a thing of the past. "Worried" writes that "vacations and leisure time are considered the greatest pleasures in life, when in fact, they should be viewed as a diversion from the most important and meaningful part–which is work." She ends her letter with the statement that "I can tell you, self-indulgence stinks. The hard-working people I know are the happiest." Interestingly, "Worried" can only associate leisure with self-indulgence. If this frame of mind represents the average person's concept of work versus leisure, then Ms. Landers' reply might possibly reflect the present folk-wisdom or advice of the "expert." Ms. Landers replied, "TGIF (Thank God It's Friday) says a lot about our culture. I cannot imagine life without work. . . . The mad scramble for leisure time says something about our values. Leisure time to do WHAT? Drink more beer? Look at more TV? Play more gin rummy? Hang out at singles bars? Somewhere along the line, work has picked up a bad name. I'd love to see it gain the respectability and prestige it once enjoyed. It's what made this country great."

Apparently, this great country's present leaders are of the same opinion. Politicians still promise to keep production up *and* at the same time, reduce unemployment. They hope to produce more and bring a steadily increasing population into the work force without a reduction of work hours. This kind of thinking results from applying outdated philosophies to modern problems.

The California Legisture recently increased the school day and school year of California students at a time when school districts are going bankrupt and quality programs have been cut to a bare minimum in the surviving districts as a direct result of Proposition 13. It's the old idea that *more* is better and *longer* is better and if it really hurts, it's the best! The more time spent toiling at a job means a better job. School is the job of the young and by all means should never be fun.

How in contrast this is to Bertram Russell's[9] essay, "In Praise of Idleness," a humorous but enlightening investigation of the work ethic in the leisure age. Russell writes that the worker does *not* consider his work the best part of his life. He will most likely not say, "I enjoy manual work because it makes me feel that I am fulfilling man's noblest task, and because I like to think how much man can transform his planet. It is true that my body demands periods of rest, which I have to fill in as best I may, but I am never so happy as when the morning comes and I can return to the toil from which my contentment springs." Russell states that he has never heard working men say this sort of thing. "They consider work, as it should be considered, a necessary means to livelihood, and it is from their leisure hours that they derive whatever happiness they may enjoy." Russell also insists that leisure is essential to education, and civilization is the product of the wise use of leisure.

But leisure frightens most people. I cannot count how many times in raising our two sons through Little League, soccer teams, music lessons, summer camps, etc., the comment was offered by other parents, "It keeps them busy and out of trouble." In this respect, the sport, the game, the lesson was not seen as an undertaking of worthiness in itself as much as it was a diversion from idleness, the "Devil's workshop." Apparently the fear that left alone a child will lapse into hanging around store fronts engaged in loathsome or illegal pursuits haunts today's parents. And perhaps with reason, but not the right reason. Persons, young and old, who do not understand leisure, who cannot handle leisure are most apt to misuse leisure time. Not realizing this most people relentlessly pursue work and other organized activities for themselves and their children. The problem, therefore, is not leisure as much as it is understanding and using leisure. Modern values are still rooted in travail.

25

The Change to Leisure Ethics

The leisure age has arrived. It is here. In a way it has been forced upon us or born to us by our own technological advancements. We are being forced to reexamine our attitudes about work and leisure in order to adapt and survive in the New Age. In a positive vein, we find ourselves at the beginning of the Leisure Revolution, one which promises man the freedom and the opportunity to finally reach his individual human potentials.

The attitude toward work, however, must be changed, not only quantitatively as in the reduction of working time, but also qualitatively. The attitude that work is only good if it hurts or if it is experienced as drudgery must be supplanted with one which incorporates more meaningful involvement and fulfillment in work. The shift is from drudgery to joyful participation. This change of attitude is crucial for the well-being of present and future generations.

Technical advancements have made it possible to distribute opportunities for leisure to all people, not only to the privileged few. Human slaves have been replaced by machine slaves, and toiling for life is no longer necessary or desirable.

History shows us again and again that leisure has been essential for the advancement of civilization because hard labor leaves no time for becoming civilized. Ironically, however, the opportunity to be at leisure is the direct result of civilization. And needless to say, the glorification of labor has always been promoted by those who did not have to spend their lives at toil or drudgery. Their only interests were in the utilitarian aspect of work and the profit derived from it. As I mentioned before, even the work ethics of ancient Greece were organized on the basis that the leisured few derived their leisure from the laboring masses.

The shift from human slave to machine slave has begun. As Isaac Asimov[10] has pointed out, there was a time when mankind faced the universe without a friend. Now he has new friends, robot creatures to help him, stronger than himself, more faithful, more useful, and absolutely devoted to him. Mankind is no longer alone.

But the question is, like so much else related to technological development, how will man use these new creatures? The solution to this problem, I think, is in the restructuring of our values. The dignity of hard labor must be replaced with the dignity of being a fine or mature human being. We must improve our participation in life. For example, we will need to rediscover some of the service professions and the inherent pride in serving—as a waiter, a cook, a social worker, a counselor, a physician, or an educator. A waiter, by being joyfully involved, will be a better waiter. He will find satisfaction in his expertise about fine foods, wines, and diet, and in his ability to speak other languages. At the same time, the public must also learn to appreciate being waited on well. People must develop the art of receiving service. It is a lot like a mutual admiration society based on attitude change and resulting in a pride in serving and a pride in being served. After all, when work is not a necessary aspect of daily human life, as it surely will not be, the pride must come from the cultivated attitude, rather than the task. And what is true about the service professions is true about all activities of living.

If we are unable to accept this challenge, I think we will face severe problems. Leontief[11] points out that societies who fail to respond to or revise their economic institutions and the accompanying values to make efficient use of changing technology, will succumb to stagnation and social disorder. They will have failed to secure the advantages for popular well-being. He also says that official computation of goods and services of the gross national product is meaningless if we fail to recognize that these benefits have also brought us increased leisure, cleaner air and purer water, aspects which greatly contribute to the well-being of working men and women. In addition, he emphasizes the fact that without leisure, the popularization of education and culture in the industrial societies of this century cannot occur.

Ginzberg[12] assigns the reasons for changes in work ethics upon the success of modern technology. It is this success that has put the super powers in the position to destroy each other and the world. This is where the true challenge lies, according to Ginzberg, not only with the respect to work, but also with regard to all human values. Youth of today has good reason to be skeptical as far as technological advancement and the future are concerned. And though we often put their contrary attitude toward work on trial, it is probably more questioning than questionable. We are resisting the change from work ethics to leisure ethics not only because it threatens long-established values, but also because we do not fully comprehend leisure.

The greatest challenge for today and for the future is in raising the consciousness level of the people to comprehend leisure. In his book, *The Next American Frontier*, Robert Reich[13] points out that the industries of the future will depend not on their hardware, but on the human software, in other words, in the qualitative aspects of human life. He says that whereas "Financial capital is highly mobile...a nation's store of human capital is relatively immobile internationally. The skills, knowledge, and capacity to work together in America's labor force will determine our collective standard of living." Again, the key is in the underlying attitude behind all human activity.

In his bestseller, *Megatrends*, John Naisbitt[14] created a new term he calls "high touch." He refers to it as the principle that symbolizes the need for balancing our physical and spiritual realities, in other words, between what we're doing and the attitude behind what we're doing.

"High tech" and the problems emerging with the new technology are already with us and the transition from the past to the future has arrived. A recent issue of *Time Magazine*[15] pointed out that two million more people in the next ten years will be employed in manufacturing, but up to sixteen million more will be employed in the service professions. And one of the greatest growth industries for the next century will be in the broad field of health and everything related to it. With this trend will come the demand for new training and expertise, with the recreation profession continuing to play a major role.

Man has entered the Age of Leisure. He is a citizen of the leisure society whether he knows it or likes it. But until his consciousness level is raised and the concept of leisure is addressed, he is doomed to frustrations and failures. The unemployed will be the slaves of subsidies. And many unknowingly liberated persons will be shackled by the accompanying sense of personal failure. Mankind's values must keep pace with the rest of his life. Classical work ethics have been outlived. The change to leisure ethics is long overdue.

26

A New Model of Leisure

As we have seen, man's concept of leisure throughout the ages has been a changing concept. How leisure has been viewed was determined by the spirit of the time. In a slave society such as the early Greeks, contemplation was sought as an ideal for the privileged few. It was the essence of culture. In an empire-building society such as Rome, where work was a necessity, the dualistic work-rest concept flourished. With the Christian focus on Divine contemplation, the dimension of spirituality and other-worldliness was added.

Gradually, manual labor became an act of humility and idleness a vestige of sin. Crafts flourished and utility was praised. Man labored to unlock the universal secrets and transform the world to suit his needs. With the rise of industry, labor reigned uppermost in the daily lives of the "industrious" citizens. Men and women worked, children labored, the masses toiled, slaves of the new-founded machinery. Work was synonymous with toil, drudgery and travail. In such a situation, leisure was viewed as a rest from work, diverted time, entertainment or amusement. In the post-industrial society where social improvements relieved man from the tediousness of long hours and despicable working conditions, work was once more made bearable. The self-prostitution of the worker was reduced. The eight-hour work day, the five-day work week, health insurance, workers' compensation, child labor laws, retirement plans, vacations, unions, etc., all helped the worker improve his lot. But still the work act itself was regarded as essentially necessary and good.

The facts that production now exceeds consumption, that the growing world population cannot possibly be absorbed into the work force, that expanding automation and advanced technology is presently replacing human labor with machine-computer-robot labor, are virtually ignored. The world cannot continue functioning under obsolete values. The *Zeitgeist* of the later twentieth century must rid itself of archaic models. The glorification of work in terms of profit and production must change to a new set of values and the human element of the person must replace the worker label.

Man treads the earth primarily as a person, not as a worker. His continuous labor simply is not needed. It is superfluous to his survival and the progress of civilization. Modern man's way of living must be rethought to accommodate his new status, his personhood. In order to do this, he needs a new model of leisure.

A model, of course, is essentially a concept formation. It has no *reality* because concepts cannot be seen or heard or smelled, or otherwise perceived. All models, though basically limited, try to give form or design to an idea. They explain in words and labels in an attempt to transmit meaning and understanding of theoretical constructs. Scientists employ this approach when they try to share their perception of reality with others. Physicists talk about such things as magnetic "fields" and gravitational "forces" and light "waves" and charged "particles" and electron "orbits" and quantum "jumps." But these phenomena are not at all what they say they are, nor do they do what the words suggest they do. Atoms do not "jump" from one quantum state to another.

The familiar model that is used to introduce children to the concept of atomic structure shows electrons orbiting around a nucleus like planets around a sun. This model can be seen in any junior high science classroom fully equipped with red protons, yellow electrons all orbiting around a big blue neutron. The model is "wrong," of course, but it is a construct which permits the young mind to somehow grasp that which cannot be seen or sensed. It is an approximation, however crude, and as such is unreal. But it permits the insights of one mind to penetrate the thinking of another. And, after all, it is with such models, comprised of crude drawings and inadequate word-labels that scientists communicate and together with great leaps of insight advance their understanding, building theory upon theory, model upon model. Niels Bohr,[16] the Nobel laureate, said, "When it comes to atoms, language can be used only as poetry. The poet, too, is not nearly as concerned with describing facts as with creating images."

And so, with this in mind, I present a new model of leisure, the *Lifestyle Attitude Model* which is compatible with the changing role of man in the twenty-first century.

27

Being Lived and Living Life

The lifestyle attitude of a person is comprised of two inter-related processes which I call *Being Lived* and *Living Life*. Before you even live life, you are being lived. That means you are being circulated, metabolized, breathed, secreted, equilibrated, and so forth. You are being lived by these processes, but do not consciously participate in them. After all, you do not start the day deciding how many milligrams of adrenalin you will produce and when you will inject it into the blood stream. The body automatically does this. It lives you. In the process of digestion, you put food into your mouth, chew it, swallow it, and the body extracts what it needs and eliminates what it doesn't need. All the glands of inner secretion and metabolic processes functioning inside the body maintain the inner balance or integrity of the organism. The body operates under the same wisdom which makes a butterfly out of a caterpillar. It is all taken care of by nature. So, therefore, you are being lived, before you are doing the living. Nature is living you and providing the very crux of your existence.

In fact, less than ten percent of the movements you perform throughout the day are initiated directly by you. As soon as you are born, even before the umbilical cord is cut, you have no other choice but to breathe. You are, throughout your life, primarily a function of your own nature and the nature around you.

Your flow of life is in constant flux. The organism is forever seeking equilibrium but never fully gaining it. The flow of energy moves toward the maintenance of the organism and the preservation of its own integrity. Lifestyle attitude is a process which might best be illustrated by vectors or mobile arrows which have movement (energy) and, as such, magnitude and direction. The word vector itself comes from the Latin word *vehere* which means "to carry." The vectors I will use will show how organisms carry themselves, the way they express their kinetic energy, and how life itself carries on.

In the following diagram, the *Being Lived* vector illustrates that part of your life which is beyond your control and which I call the *natural realm* of your lifestyle.

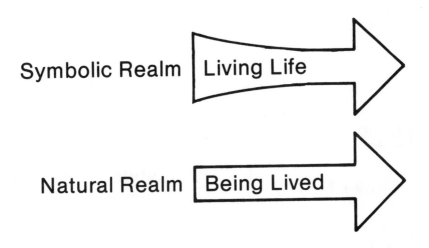

Symbolic Realm | Living Life

Natural Realm | Being Lived

The other dimension of your lifestyle is represented by the *Living Life* vector and is commonly referred to as culture. I call it the *symbolic realm* of life, where you are actually in charge of your life. When you are living life, you are making choices.

Not all functions, however, exist totally in one realm or the other. Due to the complexity of the human organism, the two basic processes are not mutually exclusive but interact in different ways. And what might originate in one realm can be transferred to the other. For instance, the digestive process originates in the realm of *Being Lived.* Yet the digestive process in humans can overlap into the symbolic realm of *Living Life*. A person can make a choice of what food to put into his mouth—the four basic food groups, some tempting junk food, maybe Italian pizza or Chinese cuisine. Chinese? Cantonese, Mandarin or Szechuan? The possibilities are endless. Add the question of *how* you should put the food into your mouth. With chopsticks or a fork? With the right hand or the left? With the fork tilted upward or downward? With a napkin around your neck or on your lap? Different cultures have different customs and rules regarding the eating process. In China, they are as concerned with the proper use of the chopsticks as Western culture is with the manipulation of the knife and fork. I lived in Persia where eating with the left hand was unthinkable. It was considered unclean since the left hand was reserved for the toilet.

Together these two dimensions, *Being Lived* and *Living Life*, illustrate the complete flow of your life, your total lifestyle attitude. This is represented in the parallel vectors wtihin the larger vector diagram below:

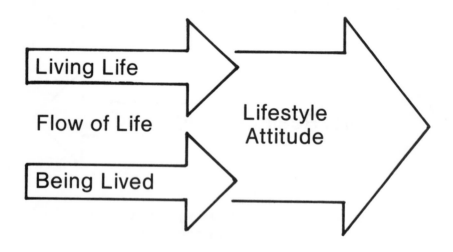

Within the interrelationship of these two basic lifestyle dimensions lies the uniqueness of human existence. Man, on one hand, is a product of nature and is controlled by it. On the other hand, he can change nature and be changed by it. In addition, of course, man can also change himself. And it is this aspect of man's condition, his ability to change himself, that is all-important.

The ability to change the way you live allows you to change your lifestyle which, in turn, changes you. Referring again to the digestive process, which was broadened to include the entire eating process, you have been taught to eat with a knife and fork. You have been taught an acceptable way to eat with a knife and fork. It has become the "right" way for you to put food into your mouth. You have also been raised not to burp and belch while sitting at the dinner table. Using the fork incorrectly or eating with a knife, or worse yet, eating with your fingers, has been met with disapproval. A parent can become very upset if the child does not follow the customs or etiquette procedures of his culture. In turn, the child who is routinely nagged about his eating manners can internalize his resentment and make himself physically ill. He could develop indigestion, an acid stomach or, in more extreme cases, an ulcer.

The *how* you eat can become more important than *what* you eat or *how much* you eat or how you are digesting and nourishing yourself. On occasion, the feeding game can upset the digestive system of children and parents alike, literally tying their stomachs into knots or interfering with the secretions and equilibrium of the body. This situation well illustrates the interdependence of the natural and symbolic realm of the human lifestyle. Depending on the mixture of the natural and symbolic aspects of the eating game, you can make yourself or others healthy, obese, undernourished, or downright neurotic. All of this is a question of harmony or disharmony between the two realms of Being Lived and Living Life.

The rest of the animal world does not have this type of problem. For animals, food intake and digestion are impulsively and naturally regulated and void of rules. The animal bends down and uses its teeth and lips to get food into the mouth. The animal knows what to eat, how much to eat, and stops eating when it is satisfied. There are no choices and definitely no values about right or wrong eating. Animals, so to speak, are being chewed, being digested, being dieted and, as such, being lived. Man's ability to choose how, when, where, and what to eat gives the whole process of food intake "meaning." Modern life is also further complicated by the psychological ploys of advertising, mass media, and product selling associated with food intake. We are all influenced early in life to purchase certain brands and products in order to reap such rewards as "the good life," sexual prowess, professional success, and so forth. Eating is no longer a natural function because food intake is vested in meaning galore. It is this symbolic dimension which separates man from the rest of nature. Ironically, for most people, the symbolic realm has taken control over their life and yet, at the same time, has given them the feeling of being "naturally" in command of their existence.

The idea that man perceives the symbolic realm as real life is not new. It has its origins in Indian philosophy of the Dravidian period which goes back as far as 5000 B.C. This basic concept is referred to as *maya,* which freely translated means "life-illusion." The concept of Maya is beautifully expressed by the well-known statue of the goddess Sakti who represents the female as projected energy of the male Siva. Their union is expressed in her cosmic dance (Lila), signifying the divine action of nature. According to Indian philosophy, the dancing Sakti is the movement of true life, or as I would say, the natural realm of life. She is surrounded by a wreath of flames, an illusion caused by the whirling of a torch. This illusory circle represents Maya, the symbolic realm of life. Maya has nothing to do with life itself, but represents the "keep your mouth over the plate" aspect of life which is indeed an illusion.

It is the product of man's higher attitudinal levels that allows him to create his own world. By analyzing, categorizing, manipulating, and explaining, he develops a false sense of precision, understanding, and control. In the process he ignores the very essence of his existence which is deeply rooted in the wholeness of nature of which he is a part. As a result, man is in danger of losing touch with nature and consequently with his own nature. The man-made values of the symbolic world depart from the laws of nature. The key to well-being and a healthy lifestyle attitude lies in the harmonious flow of *Being Lived* and *Living Life.*

28

Movement is Action-Awareness

Movement is the most basic and inclusive phenomenon of life. And lifestyle attitude is expressed in movement. Plants and lower animals move toward what is needed for their existence and away from what threatens it. They express their lifestyle attitude quantitatively and qualitatively through patterns of growth and motility which are supported by movement from within. This internal, irregular zigzag movement of particles suspended in liquid or gas is known as Brownian motion. It is present in protoplasm, the fundamental material from which all living things are composed. The movement of aqueous colloidal suspension is the source of kinetic energy of living matter. Beyond it lies the secret of life and of the process of *Being Lived.*

Being alive then is synonymous with being lived. And being lived means nothing else than moving. The same holds true for man's symbolic realm where he is living life and in charge of his own movements. Different forms of movement are expressions of the way organisms live their lives. Examples of this range from the contraction and expansion of a cell, to the movement of muscles and to the electrochemical activities involved in the process of thinking. The sum of all these various movements make up the organism's lifestyle attitude.

A plant, for instance, orients itself by light. And depending upon the other environmental circumstances, the plant develops a certain growth pattern that not only influences its growing up (leaves, branches, stems), but also its growing down (roots). The lifestyle attitudes of plants are manifested in their patterns of growth. For instance, the cypresses typical of Monterey, California, will have a completely different appearance, or in my language, will express a completely different lifestyle attitude, than a similar cypress growing in a cultivated garden.

The same is true about the lifestyle attitudes of simple animal forms. The amoeba, or single-celled animal, expresses its attitude not only in its growth pattern, but also in its movement. In fact, animals are separated from most of the plant kingdom by their ability to move. They have motility. A single animal like the amoeba is attracted or repelled by stimuli. And by the processes of gelation and solation, it moves and thereby expresses an attitude toward the respective stimulus.

Higher animals no longer just react to stimuli. They also relate emotionally to the world around them. They have an emotional life. They react to objects and are not merely attracted or repulsed by stimuli. The actions of higher animals are guided by the way they perceive an object. They are object oriented. They show their attitude toward the object by the manner in which they relate to it emotionally. They might relate with interest, delight, fear, apathy, or hostility.

Attitude, then, encompasses the whole organism and its interaction with the environment. Your lifestyle attitude is the way you are on this earth and, as such, it is the true expression of how you live your life. It is not just a way of thinking. Lifestyle attitude is a function of both action and awareness and, as such, is an expression of the whole organism. For instance, when you are timid, you not only think timid, you show timidity. It can be recognized in your movements, your face, your feelings, and your thoughts. Your attitude is truly embodied in you. To put it a different way, the body cannot be separated from the mind, nor can action be divided from awareness. They are a unit. The organism is a whole, experiences the world as a whole, and acts and reacts as a whole. The dichotomy of body and mind or the separation of action from awareness is a very unfortunate and erroneous concept. I call it the *Cartesian Curse*. Cartesius is the Latin name of the

French philosopher Rene Descartes. The theory for which he is most known is the dichotomy of physical substances and human thought or the body-mind dualism. In his philosophy, the physical universe is conceived as a mechanical system. Even the bodies of animals are automata. It is rational control which enables the soul to will what is good for the body. This basic theory goes back to Plato and St. Augustine. The mind is seen as a separate entity from the body and only housed in the brain. This separation of the body from the mind, of behavior from consciousness, is a perfect example of the deterministic Zeitgeist I spoke about earlier in the book. It separates not only the body from the mind, but the self from others, man from nature. It is an "either-or" way of looking at the world. Either right or wrong, good or bad, man or environment, self or others. This dichotomy changes the universe into a duo-verse.

Gregory Bateson,[17] in his book *Steps Toward an Ecology of Mind,* considers this dualistic world view to be a basic error in the way Western man views his existence. Many grave predicaments of modern life have their origin in this dualism. The polarized way of seeing himself and the world around him has not only estranged man from nature, but also from his own nature and the nature of others. Disease, overpopulation, wars, and pollution are products of the body-mind dichotomy. By dealing with everything as isolated entities, he has lost touch with the complementary features of his existence which make up the holistic character of the world.

In this sense, then, to separate awareness (mind) from action (body) is unrealistic, to say the least. The brain expands its neurological network throughout the body and its perceptive organs are in touch with its surroundings. Besides, the brain is dependent on the proper functioning of the rest of the organism, cultural input and environmental conditions. The separation of awareness from action should have never occurred. Processes of the mind are movements of the organism and cannot be divided without destroying the integrity of the whole. To deal with the complexities of human life in terms of outwardly manifested behavior only, ignores the existence of awareness. Action and awareness complement each other and are not mutually exclusive. Together they represent the way an organism expresses itself in the world—its lifestyle attitude.

The lifestyle attitude of the human organism is made up of the sum total of its motions, sensations, emotions, and thoughts. All are movements, and together they give the life of an individual its personal style. How you move, how you sense, how you feel, and how you think make up your lifestyle attitude. This is what I mean when I say, "you *are* your attitude."

The properties of attitude have been examined and interpreted by many modern writers. In his classic paper on attitude in 1935, the well-known psychologist, Gordon Allport,[18] made the following statement:

> The concept of attitude is probably the most distinctive and indispensable concept in contemporary social psychology....It is elastic enough to apply either to the disposition of single, isolated individuals or to broad patterns of culture.

Within the conceptual frameworks of different attitude theories, attitude not only is recognized as an indicator of action, but also as a constituent, determinant and result of it. I view attitude as a function of action and awareness and therefore a holistic expression of the organism. Action and awareness are indivisible and are manifestations of the same reality. They are integral components of attitude that are linked by continuous reciprocal involvement. They are in appearance two, but in essence one.

Lifestyle attitudes of the human organism emerge from this action-awareness or awareness-action. Both terms are appropriate as action and awareness complement each other in all aspects and are not mutually exclusive. In fact, in order to simplify the concept and make it easier to grasp, I have used the analogous expressions "body" and "head" and "action" and "awareness" interchangeably in parts of this book. Whichever terms are used, the conceptual model is the same. Lifestyle attitude is movement and movement is action-awareness.

29

Tropism and Taxis

In today's world, the most accepted scientific theory of how life came about is referred to as spontaneous chemical evolution. Scientists who researched this theory concentrated their studies on so-called nucleoproteins with autocatalystic properties, that is, nucleoproteins having the ability to bring about self-initiated chemical reactions. They learned that these proteins, at one stage of development, joined with nucleic acid and produced molecular structures which were able to duplicate their own. In order for life on this earth to start, only one such reproducible nucleoprotein was needed. The emergence of the process of reproduction, in other words, became the key to life.

In order for other forms to develop, the nucleoproteins had to change their molecular makeup and create new structures known as "mutations." Continued mutation and further aggregation of molecules eventually led to the appearance of viruses which were once considered to be living organisms. Their chemical identity now suggests, however, that they are non-living proteins, similar to the genes in the nucleus of a living cell.

In the process of evolution, the structures of viruses continued to increase in complexity. Larger types evolved, formed membranes and attracted electrolytes, fats, sugars, and other substances. As they became capable of performing more and more complex and specialized functions, they developed into bacteria which are among the smallest living organisms and are often called germs or microbes. A bacterium does not have any internal differentiation and lacks a definite nucleus. But the change from bacteria to cellular organisms was hardly a change at all since a bacterium is almost identical with the nucleus of a cell. By surrounding itself with cytoplasm, and an outer membrane, it merely added metabolic substances and enzymes.

Interestingly, all the stages between bacteria and single-celled organisms are still represented in the world today. One such unicellular animal is the amoeba, a one-celled microscopic animal studied in all high school biology classes. Although it might seem outrageous to compare and equate the amoeba with the human organism, a comparison of the two reveals many commonly shared characteristics. Both have the ability to ingest, to excrete, to metabolize, to breathe, to reproduce, and above all to move independently. Whereas photosynthesis supported the progress of bacteria into planthood, it was motility which provided the basis for their development into animalhood.

In plants, lifestyle attitude is expressed through a process called tropism. Basically, tropisms are involuntary responses to different kinds of stimuli. Geotropism, for instance, is the response of a plant to gravity. While the roots of a tree expand toward the center of the earth, the trunk and branches grow in the opposite direction. It can be said that the roots are positively geotropic and the trunk is negatively geotropic. The growth of plants is still governed by nature, except, of course, when man interferes with it. But even then they are attracted impulsively by certain stimuli and they move or grow toward those stimuli. The awareness of plants is impulsive and their action patterns are expansile, meaning they grow. The way in which the whole tree expands or how it moves becomes an expression of its tropism, its lifestyle attitude.

A tree will grow toward the light source and the roots will grow into the ground toward the water source. In a coastline climate, the roots will be deeper and better anchored because of the winds and erratic water source. Likewise, its branches will show the force or stress of the wind by being bent more inland and being more bizarrely shaped. A tree nurtured in an inland garden will have a less developed root system and a tendency to grow straighter and more regularly. So therefore, the lifestyle attitude is embodied in the tree. You can see it in the way the roots and branches have developed.

In the world of simple animals, the equivalent of tropism is called taxis. As I said before, the main difference between plants and animals is that animals have motility, the ability to move, or locomotion. A single-celled animal exhibits taxis by constantly changing the shape of its body through forming temporary extensions known as pseudopodia which means "false feet." Pseudopodia are used to move from place to place and also to capture food. Like plants, amoebae are capable of reacting to stimuli by moving either toward or away from sources such as light (phototaxis), heat (thermotaxis), chemicals (chemotaxis), gravity (geotaxis), and touch (thigmotaxis).

The origins of amoeboid movement are not yet fully understood. It seems that there are differences in surface tension, pH, or osmotic pressure between parts of the cell involved. The results are progressive processes of "gelation" and "solation" of the protoplasm in the outer layer (cortex) of the cell. This change from a jellylike substance into a liquid balloons the pseudopodium out. As the cortex becomes firm again, the pseudopodium is reabsorbed and the body of the amoeba moves forward. The amoeba continues its movement toward the stimulus as long as the stimulus is present. In the case of chemicals, movement toward a chemical is known as positive chemotaxis and movement away from the chemical, negative chemotaxes. In general terms, the difference between plants and animals is that plants exhibit growth and animals demonstrate motility. There are some exceptions in the animal world like the sponge which is considered an animal, but is tied to the ground and cannot "move." Certain slime molds are likewise considered to be plants, but they move around. But these exceptions are very few.

It can be said that these movements, expansion in plants and motility in lower animals, are their basic lifestyle attitude. The lifestyle attitude of plants is expressed through an impulsive awareness toward stimuli and the accompanying expansile action. Lower animals also demonstrate impulsive awareness, but add motile action to their repertoire. The hiatus between plants and lower animals is the change from growth to motility. Animals

103

have motile-impulsive action-awareness whereas plants have an expansile-impulsive action-awareness.

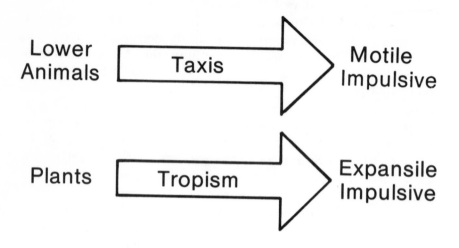

The lifestyle attitude of plants and lower animals is referred to as tropism and taxis respectively. The characteristics of tropism and taxis, namely growth and motility, are not restricted to plants and lower animals, however. They are also present on the human level in the growth of tissue and locomotion of red and white blood cells, for example.

So, lifestyle attitude is directly related to movement. The exhibition of movement in lower animals evolved during an early phase of evolution when viruses developed into more advanced molecular structures. This step is considered to be the transitional link between living and non-living matter. The fact is, being alive has become synonymous with being able to move. Where there is movement, there is life. And where there is life, there is lifestyle attitude.

30

From Motion to Emotion

Affect is to emotion as weather is to climate. Both are movements that flow through the whole organism. The part of movement which is immediately expressed and can be seen from the outside is known as affect. Affect manifests itself in the form of postures, gestures, facial grimaces, changing skin coloration, pitch or intensity of voice, reflections in the eyes and many other outwardly observable expressions. All of these movements, of course, originate from within the organism. They are the result of cellular, hormonal, cardiovascular, muscular, visceral and other changes. These changes are caused by variations in body chemistry, electrical processes, tension patterns, blood flow adjustments, and so forth. The sum total of all these outer and inner movements are commonly referred to as emotions. They are experienced as excitement, anger, happiness, anxiety, jealousy, etc. As such, they influence our moving and sensing as well as feeling and thinking.

The word "emotion" has its origin in the Latin *emotionare* which literally translated means "to move out." This outward movement or showing of emotion becomes the indication of the organism's relationship to its environment.

As you know, lower animals express their lifestyle attitude strictly through motility. They are attracted to that which is satis-

105

fying and repulsed by anything that is distressing. As such, they do not have emotion. Higher animals display their relationship with the environment through their emotions, that is, through their affective-emotive action-awareness patterns. Any form of interaction leads to contentment or displeasure and a tendency to approach or withdraw. If displeasure is eliminated and the underlying need is satisfied, the organism becomes at ease again. Between these two poles of being at ease and feeling uneasy the flow of life ensues. For example, a hungry lion will continue to be restless until its hunger is stilled. Once the belly is full, it can relax and lie in the sun.

Life is a constant fluctuation between being at ease or experiencing pleasure and feeling uneasy or experiencing pain. This pleasure-pain mechanism is referred to as hedonistic self-regulation which controls human life on the three levels of growth, motility and emotion. Together they represent man's natural realm of life. It is nature's way of living the organism.

Man is not born with emotions, however. They develop from the interaction of innately active forces within the organism and stimuli provided by the environment. Before a child is even born, it demonstrates basic reflexes and random movements without purpose or direction. We say that the fetus is alive; it moves; it is excited. But it is impossible to recognize any specific emotions at this stage of development.

Stratton[19] coined the term "undifferentiated excitement" for these early emotions that are not distinguishable. The organism is excited, but the excitement is neither pleasant nor unpleasant. No inclination as to pleasure or pain can be recognized. Generalized, undifferentiated excitement is readily visible immediately after birth. It represents the one and only emotion of the newborn.

In her genetic theory of emotions, Bridges[20] proposes that the generalized excitement gradually becomes differentiated and is associated with sensori-motor and environmental experiences to create separate emotional responses. Practically all research on the development of emotions agrees that this process is closely tied to growth. According to Bridges, the first major stratification of emotions during the early days of infancy is between distress and delight. Later, during the first two years, distress becomes further differentiated into fear, anger, and general distress whereas delight becomes further divided into joy, affection, and

106

general delight. By the age of five, more sophisticated emotions emerge such as shame, jealousy, envy, guilt, disappointment, disgust, elation or affection toward other children. This process of differentiation continues and increases in complexity throughout childhood and all the way into adulthood. The first sign of true depression, for instance, does not surface as an emotion before adolescence when aimlessness, boredom, and self-preoccupation in the young adult can be recognized. The same undifferentiated emotions of early infancy and all the acquired stages of emotions remain apparent throughout a person's life in somewhat modified form. And although the stages are more or less predictable, there is individual variation. Not everyone develops at the same rate. Physical and environmental factors also influence emotional development. Not everyone experiences the same gamut of emotions, but each person develops those consistent with his own physiological and emotional tendencies and his very personal life experiences.

The diagram below represents the evolution of emotions:

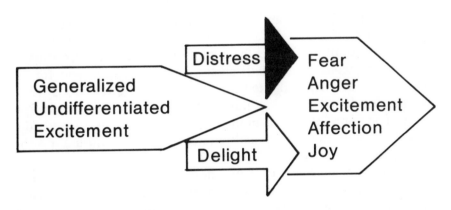

It shows the development from unspecific, random motions to the increased differentiation, sophistication and complexity of human emotions.

31

Animate Lifestyle Attitude

Most people are familiar with the evolutionary process from a one-celled life form to a human organism, or the Darwinian theory of evolution. During the evolutionary process, according to this theory, cells multiplied, clustered and created new forms. Some of these forms adapted to perform specific functions while others developed interdependent and mutually supportive systems. The complexities of multicellular structures increased continuously and eventually culminated in the evolution of the human organism.

But in spite of these complex developments from amoeba to man, some of the most fundamental principles of life have remained the same. As I described before, both a one-celled animal and a human being demonstrate their existence as living organisms through the kinetic energy of protoplasmic movement. The direction of this movement and the nature of its rhythmic contractions and expansions are the expression of *how they are* in this world. Like the amoeba, higher animals and man move throughout their lives toward or away from stimuli and exhibit different responses of tension and relaxation while doing so. This comparison applies, of course, to the very basic processes only. On these essential levels, all of the initiated movements are innate or impulsive and are a part of the total genetic make-up of all organisms. The movements of lower animals, in fact, resemble those of plants in their response to light or gravity. The orientation (motility) of certain types of fish, for example, is influenced by light and gravity very much the same as the growth of roots and branches are. If the organ of balance in the ear of a fish is removed, the fish will use light to orient itself. If the light source is placed below the tank, the fish will react by swimming upside down.

Both plants and lower animals are guided in the development of their lifestyle repertoire by specific relationships with their immediate surroundings. Consequently, their existence is restricted by stimuli. They are unable to initiate an attitude in relation to the substances and conditions with which they come in contact. The motile action of an amoeba, in other words, is not an expression of intentional motion, but rather a reaction to a stimulus. Therefore, it is impossible for lower animals to "decide" whether or not to approach or avoid a stimulus. The lifestyle attitude of plants and lower animals operates on stimulus orientation.

The next step up on the phylogenetic scale is the higher animals. Like plants and lower animals, they too are capable of growing and moving. But they have acquired another dimension, namely sensing. Whereas plants and lower animals are without choice in being attracted or repelled by stimuli, higher animals have the means of relating to their environment directly through their senses. They have object orientation. They are able to rely on their senses to relate to objects in the environment. Incoming information is evaluated by the organism on an *emotional* level and then the decision is made to either approach or avoid an object. Anything that promises to fulfill a need or is experienced as pleasureful will be approached. Anything perceived as threatening or associated with pain will be avoided. As I mentioned before, this mechanism is referred to as hedonistic self-regulation.

An amoeba cannot avoid being attracted to an outside source such as light or a specific chemical. A dog, however, can sense if he is hungry and if the food is edible or not. On the basis of his emotional reaction to the food object, he will eat or not eat it. The "decision" in other words, is his and is reflected in his lifestyle attitude. The dog can demonstrate how he relates to a situation by wagging his tail and approaching, by baring his teeth and growling, by attacking or by rolling over and exposing his belly. These reactions are all emotionally based and object oriented.

Any one of these actions is an immediately expressed and observed emotion known as affect. Only higher animals are capable of having an affective-emotive relationship to their environment. They go beyond the stimulus orientation of tropism and taxis. By extending their capabilities to object orientation, they enter a higher level which I call *Animate Lifestyle Attitude*. Animate lifestyle attitude allows organisms to relate through affective-emotive action-awareness with the objects that surround them.

What we have established is really a hierarchy of action-awareness patterns that lead to more and more sophisticated lifestyle attitudes. The most simplistic lifestyle attitude is the expansile-impulsive action-awareness of plants (tropism) characterized by growth. The next lifestyle attitude is the motile-impulsive action-awareness of lower animals (taxis) characterized by motility. And the third lifestyle attitude is the affective-emotive action-awareness of higher animals (animate) characterized by emotion. The advancement from stimulus to object orientation or impulse to emotion is the hiatus between lower and higher animals. All three levels represent the animalistic or natural world of man — the one that lives him, or as I said earlier, the one he is being lived by.

The diagram below illustrates the development of lifestyle attitudes of animal organisms:

ACTION-AWARENESS: LIFESTYLE ATTITUDE:

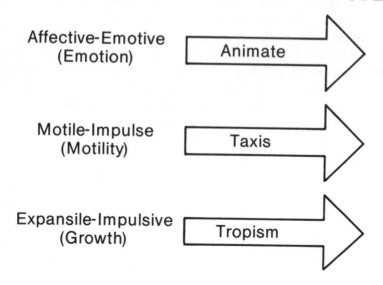

Affective-Emotive (Emotion) — Animate

Motile-Impulse (Motility) — Taxis

Expansile-Impulsive (Growth) — Tropism

Human beings and higher animals react to each other as well as to conditions in their external environment. The respective reactions find their expressions in the inner and outer movements of the organism. An organism, in other words, demonstrates the way it is on this earth, its lifestyle attitude, through its patterns of growth, motility and emotion. By being able to react emotionally to different situations and objects, the attitudinal level of higher animals extends beyond tropism and taxis to animate attitude.

Certain impulsive patterns of action-awareness are commonly referred to as drives or instincts. The character of drives is determined by an animal's evolutionary heritage and is dependent upon specific internal and external conditions. Unlimited examples can be found in migratory and reproductive expressions which depend on the highly complex interplay of hormonal and environmental influences. During the mating time, the animal is impulsively driven until the instinctual message is fulfilled.

Within the animate lifestyle attitude of higher animals is found the most basic form of play. When scarcity is not an immediate problem for the animal, when it is not driven by any unsatisfied need for survival, it can play. The animal's play is based on feelings of satisfaction and contentment in the moment. After feasting on his prey, the lion plays with the cub. After eating the picnic droppings, the squirrels chase each other and frolic. The flow of life takes place within the balance of satisfaction and dissatisfaction, restlessness and contentment.

Higher animals relate emotionally to the world by sensing, but are basically still "being lived." They are governed by nature through pleasure-pain response mechanisms, that is, through hedonistic self-regulatory processes. Or in simpler terms, the head is in service of the body.

Man, as I have said before, has another dimension to his existence. Besides being lived, he is also capable of living life. His basic existence is very deeply rooted in the natural realm. It keeps him, so to speak, under the umbrella of nature which protects him, maintains him, and altogether lives him. He cannot fully escape from the umbrella, however, because he is bound by his animate lifestyle attitude. Nevertheless, he has developed ways of getting out from under it by creating culture, the symbolic realm. Human beings, in other words, are not only acted on by nature and react to it like the rest of the animal world, but they also have the ability to act on nature. This added lifestyle dimension is uniquely human. It is represented in my model by three additional attitudes that reach far beyond the animate lifestyle attitude.

111

32

The Emergence of the Person

What does it mean to be human? Man's discovery of his existence as a person, that is, a separate entity from the rest of the world, originates from his awareness of his own actions. During the early stages of infancy, this self-discovery process becomes very apparent. The infant continuously examines and tests his environment through various forms of interaction. Objects are put into the mouth, touched, looked at, listened to or thrown out of the crib. Through the input and processing of a multitude of signals, specific neural sequences are created in the brain which form complex action-awareness patterns. These new patterns become the basis for the establishment of higher lifestyle attitudes in man. It is an incredibly complex process considering that at birth and shortly afterwards, man is strictly being lived by the most primitive part of the brain, the brain stem. In fact, the brain stem is present in all vertebrates from reptiles all the way up to man. And therefore it is often referred to as the reptilian brain.

During his first days of existence, the infant is governed solely by this structure and has little more neural equipment at its disposal than a reptile has. According to the well-known physiologist, Delgado,[21] there are no detectable signs of mental activity at birth and, in this respect, human beings are born without a mind.

Altmann[22] proclaims that only twenty percent of the normal complement of nerve cells in the organism are present in the cerebral cortex at birth. The other eighty or ninety percent appear during infancy under specific conditions and these conditions are mainly directed by stages of genetically determined readiness levels and sensory input. In other words, they are dependent on the interaction between an active organism and its environment.

The next and more highly developed layer in the brain is known as the limbic system. It used to be referred to as the rhinencephalon or nose-brain, literally named because the neural center for the sense of smell is located in it. The limbic system is found in all mammals. The most important part of this system, according to MacLean,[23] is the hypothalamus. In his research he found it by accident to be the pleasure center of the organism. In the 1940's, Walter Hess[24] conducted experiments with electrical stimulation of the brain and found the limbic system to be the center of the rage response and the coordination of flight and fight reactions. Many more studies have been conducted since, and have reaffirmed this part of the brain to be the seat of the emotions which selects neural sequences on the basis of pleasure and pain experiences. The earliest action-awareness patterns are created by these hedonistic self-regulatory processes. We are born only with a set of genes which carry practically unlimited potential for self-development. But this potential must be stimulated in order to grow. It will not fully develop on its own.

The child, then, is really a sensory system which senses incoming stimuli from the environment and connects them with the pleasure areas inside the brain. The repetition of experiences establishes neural sequences in the central nervous system that become the very essence of the lifestyle attitude of the child.

One of the first works concerning the attitudinal development during the early stages of human growth was published in 1863 by the renowned Russian physiologist, Sechenow.[25] His book, *Reflexes of the Brain,* offers fascinating insights into the early life of the newborn child. He stresses specifically the importance of sensory stimulation to all activities, from the movement of the limbs to the process of thinking. He feels the initial cause of every action stems from external sensory stimulation. Such sensory activity is a basic life-sustaining process. Together with the spontaneous activity of the organism, it is expressed in movement which in turn maintains the integrity of the organism. It is the body's basic striving for life, regulated by approaching sources favorable for survival and satisfaction and avoiding or withdrawing from sources which are threatening or distressful.

According to Sechenow, man is born with a tiny number of instinctive movements. He can open and close his eyes, suck, swallow, scream, cry, hiccup, and sneeze. The sphere of sensations in the newborn child is also limited because the infant cannot really see, hear, smell, or touch. These acts require the activity of definite groups of muscles which cannot be controlled by the newborn child. Sechenow also points out that at the beginning of human life, reflexes without exception are of an emotional character.

The child does not react passively to external influences. Instead the child actively strives toward the outer world and this striving is the most basic phenomenon of life. The complete dependence on these explorations is responsible for the continuous activities of the child which constantly pass from the exercise of one nerve to another. This process contributes to the all-around development of the sense organs and to the maturation of the movements of the organism.

Piaget[26] demonstrated in his research that shortly after birth an infant cannot tell the difference between himself and his environment. In fact, the body of the mother is much closer to him than parts of his own body. He feels at one with the breast and the nipple and all that he senses and feels in association with them. Whatever he perceives of himself and his immediate environment is united under the umbrella of nature. Boundaries between the "I" and the world out there have not yet been established in the child's action-awareness patterns. His experiences are truly holistic. Piaget refers to this phenomenon as protoplasmic consciousness. From it, the child moves through several clearly defined developmental periods toward autonomy.

In order to recognize oneself as an autonomous being, the process of thinking has to be developed to higher levels. Piaget points out that awareness of our own thought process makes it possible to separate *ourselves* from our environment. Knowing that we think of things detaches us from the actual thing. Piaget[27] studied the maturation of thought in children. The young child, he maintains, knows nothing of the nature of thought. He cannot distin-

114

guish between thought and the thing thought about. For him they are one. Inanimate objects appear to him as possessing thoughts, feelings and a will of their own. This is apparent from the artwork of small children in which the sun has a face and looks down upon the scene in the picture. Primitive peoples share this child-like view of the universe as reflected in their art, rites, and customs. Not only does the sun, moon, rain, etc., have a "life" and "will" of their own, they can be magically influenced by the will of man. Herein lies the origin of ancient deities, rites such as rain dances, and most superstitions.

To the child the external and internal world is one and the universe is under the command of the self. He possesses an egocentricity based on his inability to separate himself from his environment. He is not conscious of self. He makes his own truth and reality which he assumes is the same as every other person's truth and reality. The child feels before he thinks.

In fact, the thinking of children is first closely associated with muscular activity. The young child manipulates objects, constructs and destroys them. There is a connection between this manual activity and the thought process, or between motor activity (action) and thinking (awareness). Piaget[28] maintains that mental processes are continuations of inborn motor activities. He also introduces the concept that actions as well as thoughts are organized spontaneously and in a logical manner. He divides the development of a child's thought process into four sequential phases. Each period follows an inflexible sequence of development which is genetically programmed. But the learning of one period does overlap and functions in the subsequent phase. This means the style of thinking in earlier periods can also exist in a later, more sophisticated phase.

PIAGET'S PERIODS OF COGNITIVE DEVELOPMENT:

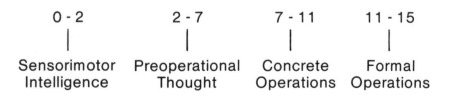

0 - 2	2 - 7	7 - 11	11 - 15
Sensorimotor Intelligence	Preoperational Thought	Concrete Operations	Formal Operations

The organism functions first through its fundamental neural formations such as the brain stem and the limbic system. They provide for a well-functioning sensory system which responds to sensory input by being attracted to satisfying sources and repulsed by distressing ones. By processing the incoming information, specific neural sequences are created which form patterns of moving and sensing and eventually of feeling and thinking. At one point during the developmental process, the child's perception of the movements of his own muscles leads to the insight that "I" am the one that moves. The organism senses its own movement through proprioceptive kinesthetic sensations and intuitively feels himself a separate entity from the world. Being conscious of one's self is the key to being human.

In the ability to reverse the order, from feeling and thinking to moving and sensing, lies the critical point which marks the start of a person. It depends on sufficient cortical maturation to have new impulses travel from moving to sensing to feeling to thinking sequences and then the other way around, from thinking to feeling to sensing to moving. The human infant's striving for sensory stimulation becomes more and more highly refined and his basic emotional expressions develop into more abstract ones. Direct approach and avoidance responses give room to wishes, desires, and longings and eventually to more sophisticated and creative thought processes. The ability to switch from a sequence of moving to thinking to one of thinking to moving marks the emergence of a person.

33

Analytic Lifestyle Attitude

From the moment of conception, man is being lived by nature. He is acted on before he actually is capable of acting on his own behalf. In the process of growing up, man moves from an essentially impulsive existence to one with increasing free choice. His early awareness is concentrated in actions focused upon his survival. He gradually matures and discovers not only the self, but others, and also the elements of his environment. He discovers time which permits him to venture back into the past and ahead into the future. He can mull over past events and anticipate future ones. His acquisition of language provides him with the ability to adopt the experiences of previous generations. And so, a world ruled by blind necessity turns into a world of freedom. Man's freedom, however, is not without strings attached. By gaining his freedom, he changes from a natural being into a moral being. He discovers responsibility.

Animals do not have freedom. They live under the constraint of nature. Nature calls the shots. Time is not within them. They are within time. They cannot ponder whether or not there will be enough to eat in the days ahead. For them there is no tomorrow, nor was there a yesterday. They cannot plan ahead, nor can they lose themselves in the past. They do not have language or other symbolic meanings in their life. They cannot escape the present and are unable to worry. Walt Whitman[29] expresses this idea so beautifully in his poem, "Leaves of Grass":

I think I could turn and live with animals, they are so
  placid and self-contained,
I stand and look at them long and long.
They do not sweat and whine about their condition,
They do not lie awake in the dark and weep for their
  sins,
They do not make me sick discussing their duty to God,
No one is dissatisfied — not one is demented with the
  mania of owning things,
No one kneels to another, nor to his kind that lived
  thousands of years ago,
Not one is respectable or unhappy over the whole earth.
So they show their relations to me and I accept them,
They bring me tokens of myself,
They invince them plainly in their possession,
I wonder where they got those tokens,
Did I pass that way huge times ago and negligently drop
  them?

Yes, man did pass that way huge times ago. But he did not drop those tokens. He still has them in his possession as is evident within the natural realm of his life. What man did drop was his complete surrender to nature. But in so doing, he gained something new. He discovered himself as a separate entity, as a person, and developed a sense for time and language. With these tools he created his own world and added the symbolic realm to his life. Within this realm, he gained control over his destiny. He can invent new things or ideas. He can listen in on life, explain it, manipulate it, change it. Man can make use of the artifacts and experiences of people who lived long before him. He can learn from the past, plan for the future, and pass on his insights to future generations. I call this new dimension *Analytic Lifestyle Attitude.*

Analytic lifestyle attitude is uniquely human. It is characterized by the emergence of the higher integrative functions such as the ability to anticipate, to reminisce, to imagine, to create, to judge, and to reason. The major characteristic of analytic awareness is that man goes beyond living solely in the here and now and becomes aware of the past and future. His analytic lifestyle attitude is the result of the development of cortical-rational action-awareness patterns which allow him to go beyond nature through

118

thinking. Man has progressed from an existence based on moving and sensing to one of thinking. He has moved more and more into his head. He rationalizes and reasons, explains and justifies. He creates his own world which often does not exist in reality except in his head. This offers man many options and advantages, but also poses a major threat to his life. Living too much in the head creates uneasiness. But the uneasiness is not the result of direct experience as much as it is the consequence of thought.

Uneasiness is not altogether bad because it can also be the basis for taking action. You anticipate; you take action. In fact, a certain degree of uneasiness or tension is necessary in order to grow, to learn, to mature. Even anxiousness can have positive results. A swimmer before he gets off the starting block or an actor before he steps on stage experiences start fever or stage fright, but it helps him to gear up for top performance. The same holds true for all forms of excitement. You can be positively excited. The key is in the balance between tension and relaxation. For growth, in order to maintain the flow of life, we need alternating states of tension and relaxation.

Animals are incapable of leaving their natural domain. They are exclusively lived by nature's wisdom which regulates the lifestyles of all living things. And their existence remains in harmony with nature throughout their lives. Man, on the other hand, can step out of nature and create his own symbolic world, his culture. This process was made possible through the evolution of his analytic lifestyle attitude.

The diagram below summarizes the model we have been discussing.

Person • Symbolic Realm • Thinking
Analytic Lifestyle Attitude
Time Within • Rational-Cortical • Reason

Animal • Natural Realm • Sensing
Animate Lifestyle Attitude
Within Time • Emotive-Affective • Emotion

119

The acquisition of the analytic lifestyle attitude, however, has brought other less desirable aspects into man's life. He has the ability to perceive himself as a separate entity on earth, but he now is prone to thoughts of isolation and loneliness. He may be able to think about the future and the past, but he now worries about what might happen, and what could have happened. He is preoccupied with anticipation and retrospection which prevent him from experiencing the here and now. The more he lives in his head, the more he loses touch with his body. Even in the physically intimate act of intercourse, a man might still keep a record. He is "scoring" which says it completely. He's putting another notch into the bedpost. He is either focused on the end product of orgasm or even more remotely on the symbolic end product of the "final score" and all its personal and social implications. He doesn't feel his partner, sense her, smell her. Focused on the end product, he misses the process. It's a total headtrip.

Thinking, considered to be man's strength, becomes his handicap. It prevents him from experiencing the present and creates a life of anxiety and dread. Even man's language limits rather than frees him. The milieu of his symbolic world shapes him like water shapes the fish. Emerged in an ocean of words and symbols, he participates in the perpetuation of his culture without even knowing it.

This process can also work the other way around. The excitement of finding a new concept can be very physical or sensual. I'm truly physically excited when I discover a new idea or see a relationship that never existed for me before. Sometimes very heady experiences still can be grounded with the body and sometimes very physical experiences can be completely blocked by the head.

Unfortunately, modern man's life is thoroughly dominated by thought. He lives in his head. Everything is analyzed. You ask yourself, *Why did I do this? Should I do that? Could I have done something else?* The more you ask, the more questions you end up with. Most of them cannot be answered. What you are thinking about has often already happened and cannot be changed. Or, what you are preoccupied with has not yet occurred and never will. All of your action is invented in your head. All movement is cerebral and the body cannot act. It can only *react*. And this has a direct impact on your emotions. You react emotionally to thoughts that are not grounded in the present. You don't really know how you feel. You are only thinking that you should feel a certain way. For one reason or another, you make your life and perhaps the lives of others miserable. You have lost touch with yourself and with the present world. Free-floating thought and reactive emotions are a deadly combination. The pride of man, his analytic lifestyle attitude, has become a threat to his very existence.

34

Emotion, Scarcity and Toil

Is there a way out? In order to answer this question, we must have another look at human emotions. Emotions are differentiated not only by type, but also by their direction and level of intensity. First of all, organisms operate essentially on three energy levels. The first level is *low intensity* and characterized by *placidity*. When placid, the organism is at ease, relaxed, tranquil, asleep, quiet, calm, peaceful, satisfied, content, restful, complacent, or serene.

The next level is *elevated intensity* which is characterized by excitement. The organism is aroused. He experiences increased activity of generalized, undifferentiated movement. This energy level, marked by excitement, can have two near-opposite types or subdivisions. On the one hand, the excitement can be marked by *vitality*. A person may feel elated, energetic, vigorous, joyful, happy, playful, lively, vibrant, lusty, or vivacious. On the other hand, excitement may be characterized by *anxiety*. A person may feel uneasy, nervous, restless, worried, upset, apprehensive, annoyed, bothered, irritated, dissatisfied, or frustrated.

The third energy level is *high intensity* characterized by agitation. Agitation, too, can be further subdivided into *fear* and *aggression*. A fearful person may be afraid, withdrawn, scared, frightened,

122

terrified, horrified, stunned, stupefied, shocked, paralyzed, autistic, catatonic, or filled with dread. An aggressive person may be angry, irate, infuriated, raging, raving, furious, ferocious, savage, brutal, cruel, or vicious.

And so, from the three basic intensity levels—*low, elevated,* and *high*—are produced five essential emotional levels: placidity, vitality, anxiety, fear, and aggression. They constitute the basis for the vast array of recognizable human emotions.

These five emotions also have direction which is expressed in various movements depending upon the situation. The placid organism does not originate movement on its own. It is passive or neutral. It goes *with* the flow of life situations. The vital organism participates in life situations through cooperation and support. Its direction is *toward* the situation. The anxious organism is hesitating, vacillating, or driven. Its movement pattern is unstable, directed both *to* and *from* a situation. The fearful organism flees or withdraws. It moves *away* from a situation, either by running away or withdrawing within. Lastly, the aggressive organism is attacking or threatening. The movement is *against* the situation or the person himself. So each emotion implies characteristic direction and "moves out" accordingly.

Somewhere between the low-intensity level of vitality and the elevated level of anxiety is the zone of undifferentiated excitement which divides the emotions associated with either *ease* or *dis-ease.* This concept is illustrated by the diagram below:

	TYPE:	DIRECTION:	INTENSITY:
	Aggression	against	high
Crisis	Fear	away from	high
Emotions	Anxiety	to and from	elevated
Comfort	Placidity	with	low
Emotions	Vitality	toward	elevated
			high

The emotions derived from feelings of ease, I call *Comfort Emotions.* Those acquired from feelings of dis-ease, I call *Crisis Emotions.*

Let's look first at the crisis emotions. As I pointed out earlier, the "crisis reaction" has been retained by man from his evolutionary past where it very successfully helped him cope with threatening situations. Like animals, man is equipped with hormonal and metabolic responses which permit him to emotionally react to environmental threats such as natural enemies. When a man feels threatened, his adrenal gland activates and produces adrenalin which stirs him to flee or fight. It is a source of natural energy and alertness which makes him immediately responsive to the threat. Patterns known as the fight or flight response provide instantaneous mobilization of a variety of resources within the body to resolve real conflicts. The pituitary gland releases a stress hormone (ACTH) which activates the adrenal glands. Two major types of adrenocortical hormones are mineralocorticoids and glucocorticoids. Mineralocorticoids affect the electrolytes of the extracellular fluids particularly chloride, sodium, and potassium. But the full impact on the fundamental building unit of living organisms, the cell, is not yet understood. Nevertheless, its link to disease has been clearly established. Large doses of glucocorticoids reduce and sometimes even block antibody formation. This too affects a critical somatic mechanism, namely the immune system.

By continually living under free-floating anxiety and aggression, man is physically poisoning himself. Changes on cellular levels, in muscular tension, blood flow patterns, body chemistry, and so forth, all lead to dis-ease. The Harvard physiologist Walter Cannon,[30] together with Hans Selye,[31] the founder of stress research, have proven that psychological strain can cause dramatic hormonal changes and the subsequent physiological symptoms. Selye showed that long term crisis reaction patterns initiate changes in the organism which lead to high blood pressure, peptic ulcers, insomnia, arteriosclerosis, deficiencies in the immune system, and a vast variety of other manifestations of dis-ease. As we know, cancer is a basic cellular breakdown in which the process regulating cell growth no longer functions properly. The cells proliferate and eventually interfere with the life-sustaining functions of the organism. It is becoming more and more evident that stress is a major contributor to cancer, lung diseases, cirrhosis of the liver, heart disease, "accidental" injuries, and suicide. The link from chronic crisis emotions to chemical reactions in the body, to

124

cellular changes to dis-ease is recognizable. In fact, a new field, psychoneuroimmunology, has been created to explore the way emotional states affect the body defenses.

The crisis reaction has been an advantage to man's survival throughout the ages. Man's relationship to his environment has always been threatening to him. In order to survive, he has had to fight for basic necessities like food and shelter. The environment has been the enemy, something to fight against or run away from. For centuries, man has structured his daily life and cultural patterns around the pursuit of basic necessity. And this struggle for existence has been dominated by natural scarcity and the activation of the crisis emotions.

Scarcity has been and is the driving force behind human existence. Until very recently, scarcity has been natural or very real. Will there be enough food for the day, for the winter? Will there be enough water for thirst, for crops? Will there be enough people to labor for all the work that must be done? Drought, famine, plague, natural calamities and disasters of every sort were a constant source of scarcity. And they were very real. They threatened man's survival. Consequently, man committed his life to toil. It was do or die. And his culture consequently promoted ideals and ethics glorifying that which was necessary for survival.

Man's life is no longer dominated by natural scarcities. His existence has become more complex. Today man is controlled by artificial scarcity. Once a phenomenon of the natural realm, scarcity has been extended into the symbolic realm. It is man-made. The social organization of toil, of man's dominance over man, produces artificial scarcities. It permits a few ultra-powerful persons and corporations to organize the power structure and promote the accompanying philosophies that enslave the unsuspecting, powerless masses. Status and the demands and values of culture perpetuate artificial scarcity. The bottom line is that man spends most of his life repressing his natural urges, pleasures, and gratifications. He does not pleasurefully live in the moment, developing himself, satisfying his needs, enjoying life. Instead he is involved, often unknowingly, in a system organized by power structures like the military-industrial complex which promote values based on artificial scarcity.

Just as there is artificial scarcity, there is artificial toil. The most glaring example is in the area of shelter, put into modern terms, the housing industry. A large percentage of every person's income is used to make payments on his "home." This is one of the chief reasons people go off to work their eight-hour days, five-day weeks, forty-year careers – to pay off the mortgage. "I owe, I owe, so off to work I go" was a tragi-comic bumper stricker I saw the other day. Yet the very construction of homes by present methods is artificial toil. Frame houses, built of wood, shingles, tiles, brick, constructed from the ground up, from the outside in, and costing tens and hundreds of thousands for a few hundred square feet of living area is a remnant of pre-technological society. It is still nothing more than a glorified log cabin. Prefabricated structures, geodesic domes, and other modern methods and materials are taboo. Such inexpensive and readily available techniques would remove large numbers of construction workers from the work force. Likewise, painting by brush rather than spray gun or roller by union painters is another example of artificial labor. It is a means of keeping painters painting and as such *controlled* through work. For a long time the robotization of the auto industry has been resisted. Keeping auto workers working and hence, controlled, is the reason. Yet the second biggest expenditure of the average person is his car. He owes, he owes, so off to work he goes. We are technologically advanced enough to produce a vehicle which would cost a fraction of what the average car does. But to do so would lay off too many "workers."

And the oil industry. The gas combustion engine, the consumption of trillion of gallons, that is dollars, of oil products is also obsolete, yet how many persons would be "out of work" if the industry collapsed? And the list is endless. Artificial toil keeps us busy and the power of man over man keeps us controlled. The point is, sooner or later, this way of living cannot continue for the simple fact that it does not need to continue. Presently, the worker is at least as afraid of leisure as people in power are. He needs the job even more than the money. Both controller and worker sense that they are obsolete and this realization in itself is demeaning. A union housepainter surely does not paint his own home with a brush. He buys a spray gun. When he goes to work he knows he prostitutes himself by using a brush and this brings meaninglessness into his labor.

We cannot change from a work ethic to a leisure ethic overnight because we have not yet designed the means to cope with non-

126

laboring people. We have only tried to mend and patch present programs and systems to stave off the inevitable. The time is here to revise our thinking and our way of life.

We must recognize that artificial scarcities are self created. They are not natural. Yet we are so deeply involved in archaic, irrelevant value systems and contrived scarcities that we believe them to be real. The material surpluses, the status symbols, unnecessary labor, economic practices, and political systems to which the masses subscribe have all been imposed upon them.

Modern life is predominantly lived in the analytic attitude, and under the influence of the crisis emotions. The chronic mobilization of crisis reactions causes the organism to be constantly flooded with substances that are designed for rare life-threatening situations. Having the ability to produce "danger" in the head, man can live his entire life in a state of crisis. He poisons himself with an overdose of crisis emotions induced by self-imposed scarcity and toil.

35

The Comfort Emotions

Just as there is a connection between the crisis emotions and dis-ease, there is also a link between the comfort emotions and ease or well-being. This concept has been the cornerstone of the recreation movement. Hereto "fun" has only been associated with non-productive endeavors and has had no respectability in the "seriousness" of life. Fun has been linked to frivolity, irresponsibility, entertainment, "letting loose," and other non-serious pursuits. But the concept of fun as used in recreation is representative of all the comfort emotions. It is fun to feel good about yourself and about others; it is fun to love and be loved; it is as much fun to be alone as it is to be in the midst of people. It is fun to enjoy nature and it is fun to take care of the natural environment. "Life is great, be in it" is the slogan of the Australian Recreation movement. It means that the best way for man to live his life, including work and "serious" duties, is with the support of comfort emotions. It is natural for man to have fun. He has all the physical, intellectual, and emotional equipment to partake in fun.

The sensual aspects of man's basic needs for food, shelter, and procreation have long been enjoyed by the privileged, but for the masses they have been suppressed by society for strictly utilitarian purposes. The end products or goals of our efforts have most of the time been enjoyed, but the process has been marked by drudgery. We need only remember what we learned as children in the story of "The Three Little Pigs." The two little pigs who hastily dismissed the rigors of building their homes in order to sing and dance were left vulnerable to the big bad wolf. I can still see the facial expressions of those pig faces in my own childhood book. Did the "wise" little pig ever look joyful as he built his house of mortar and brick? His brows were knitted earnestly as he lay stone upon stone. And the two foolish pigs, I can see their heads thrown back, eyes closed in rapture, as they frittered their days away in song and dance. A very subtle message is contained in these pages. Joy is associated with non-productivity while drudgery is aligned with productivity. The association of joy with productivity is unthinkable. Anything that is fun and brings intrinsic rewards is frivolous and selfish and as such cannot result in anything worthwhile. Success and meaning are directly dependent on "paying the price" and suffering.

One book that associates joy with a worthwhile and productive activity was the culinary classic, *The Joy of Cooking.* It suggests that joy can be found not only in the consumption of the food, but also in the preparation and presentation of it. And still the end product, a gourmet dish, is very worthwhile. Likewise, in *The Joy of Running,* joy can be found in the run, not only in the goals of winning, cardiovascular endurance, or weight loss. And in the infamous, *The Joy of Sex,* it is permissible to find joy in the sex act itself without the end product of conception. The emphasis is on the process, which in spite of being fun, may bring about an even better end product.

Comfort emotions are process oriented. They exist in the moment and are savored because they feel good to the person. As such they are positive emotions and open to sensuousness and intuition. As pointed out before, they range from variations of placidity like being asleep, satisfied and tranquil to variations of vitality like being energetic, playful or vibrant. They soothe, heal and inspire health.

The old adage "laughter is the best medicine" is more than offhanded folk wisdom. It is a truth. There have been many studies and theories of laughter, from as far back as Aristotle and Cicero to Descartes, Francis Bacon, Hobbes, and Freud to the more recent Bergson, Beerbohm, and McDougall, to name a few. In

Spencer's[32] "Physiology of Laughter," written in 1860, he states "nervous energy always tends to beget muscular motion; and when it rises to a certain intensity always does beget it." Why excess energies are released in the form of laughter rather than another physical manner like wiggling the ears or shaking the hands has also been explored. Freud[33] notes that the smile which is the basic gesture in laughter is the primal contortion which characterizes sucklings after quitting to nurse. They are satiated, and filled with pleasure and the corners of their mouth form the grimace of a smile. Laughter, its accompanying breathing spasms, thigh slapping and foot stomping, appear to be the logical pathways to expend surplus energies or tensions. No matter what the etiology or evolution of the laughter reflex, it can be wholeheartedly embraced that laughter *feels good*.

The comfort emotions are very healthy. A most interesting article, "Anatomy of an Illness," was published in the *New England Journal of Medicine* by the well-known author, Norman Cousins.[34] In this article he explains how he literally laughed himself back to health after having been diagnosed as incurably ill from the crippling disease, ankylosing spondylitis. Cousins based his self-cure on the supposition that if negative emotions produce negative chemical changes in the body, then positive emotions produce positive chemical reactions. With that simple hypothesis, he began a daily regimen which utilized affirmative emotion, with laughter being a major ingredient. He also incorporated love, hope, faith, confidence, humor, joy, and the will to live. He watched amusing movies, tapes of Alan Funt's "Candid Camera" favorites, and noticed that ten minutes of hearty laughter acted like an anesthetic permitting him to sleep soundly for several hours. He read volumes of humorous, light-hearted, and witty books. And he got well. His body healed. In his own words, "I learned never to underestimate the capacity of the human mind to regenerate...The life-force may be the least understood force on earth...Protecting and cherishing the natural drive may well represent the finest exercise of human freedom."

Scattered accounts of persons like Cousins who "beat the odds" so to speak, exist. Faith healing, miracle cures at shrines such as Lourdes, strong wills of determined individuals, whatever the source, we all recognize the fact that some individuals have somehow unlocked the key to healing and the betterment of their lives.

The life-force or natural drive to which Cousins refers, however, is within us all. It exists as certainly as the power to hurt or destroy ourselves does. The comfort emotions are as powerful and influential as the crisis emotions. This positive life force is the *missing link* between the animate and the analytic lifestyle attitudes and is the key to health and joyful living. I call it the *Recreative Lifestyle Attitude.*

36

The Recreative Lifestyle Attitude

The Recreative Lifestyle Attitude is the missing link in man's lifestyle repertoire. He has to rediscover it in order to survive. It closes the gap between the animate and analytic lifestyle attitudes. It bridges sensing and thinking with feeling. The recreative lifestyle attitude provides equal opportunity for thinking with the body, or relating sensuously to the world and sensing with the head, or relating intuitively to the world. The recreative lifestyle attitude has sensuous-intuitive action-awareness. The head is in concert with the body.

I said we must rediscover the recreative lifestyle attitude. We all had it when we were young. A child's lifestyle attitude is much more recreative than analytic. Toys are taken apart right now, to satisfy curiosity right now, to enjoy the moment.

Before the child is able to use language, it relates to the world mainly through grasping, visual examination, tactile explorations, etc. Sensory-motor skills are achieved before readiness for language. With development of language, the emergence of the self, and the realization of space and time, the experiences of life shift from perceptions of fantasy to objectivity. This is really the core of what is called "growing up."

"Growing up" is a misleading term if it entails passing up the recreative lifestyle attitude and embracing the pure analytic. Perhaps "growing to" is better. The process of maturing should be a growing to the perfect balance of analytic and recreative lifestyle attitudes, each servicing man to complete personhood.

Not all of life's actions are based on utility. When you live with a recreative lifestyle attitude, you are not preoccupied with a goal. Utility, the great idol of the modern world, is not your target. Instead you lose yourself in the process. You do things "for the heck of it" or just because it feels good, not "because." You allow yourself to operate on an experiential level. You are involved in beautiful moving, sensing, feeling and even thinking. Peace, beauty, and freedom are the products of the aesthetic dimension which is the true center of culture. It is where the senses and the intellect meet. It is the play sphere, the vehicle toward genuine liberation, toward an existence with a minimum of destructive crisis emotions. As the Dutch philosopher, Huizinga,[35] said, "Play precedes culture."

Modern man spends his life almost exclusively in the analytic lifestyle attitude, governed by crisis emotions. His head dominates the body. Bothered by free floating anxiety and aggression, he is victimized by his self-created stress and is unable to escape. The chronic mobilization of crisis emotion patterns keeps him in a state of dis-ease.

Of course, the analytic lifestyle attitude is part of being human. It has helped man improve the quality of his existence throughout the ages. After all, part of being human is being able to plan ahead and consider past experiences. Also, without a certain amount of stress, pain, or struggle, there could be no growth, no maturation. Growing up hurts, but staying the same hurts more!

What man needs is to balance his analytic lifestyle attitude with his recreative. The recreative lifestyle attitude is present-centered and based on comfort emotions. You live here and you live now. You allow yourself to be engaged in the moment. You're not thinking of what you should do or could have done. You experience yourself and your environment and build on those experiences rather than on preconceived ideas that often are not even real.

Touch, taste, smell, listen, move, and look for yourself. Be yourself. Be responsible, that is, respond to the world and respond to yourself. Go with the kind of feelings and thoughts that are rewarding. Follow your interests. Be responsive to the interests of others. Enjoy whatever you choose to do or not to do. Have fun. Fun and joy are not dirty words. As a matter of fact, work will be more productive when you have fun doing it and when you feel good about it.

We must overcome the programming of our society that only what hurts is worth doing. Business and industry are finding out that happy, involved employees who are rewarded are far superior to plodding, diligent ones who are controlled by punishment. Just recently, two successful books on management, *The Search for Excellence*[36] and *The Art of Japanese Management,*[37] have recognized aspects of the recreative lifestyle attitude as essential to successful operations in business and industry. They speak of the importance of intrinsic motivation, of feelings of belonging and camaraderie, of the advantages of reward over punishment, and the development of the intuitive-creative side of employees. They are true proponents of the leisure ethics in classical work settings. They call for meaning and satisfaction in life within the work process and not through the end product only.

The recreative lifestyle attitude is characterized by comfort emotions, from being restful and at ease to being excited, elated, and ecstatic. The beauty of "doing nothing" can be enjoyed as much as the energy output of skiing in three feet of powder snow or working in the garden. In its most highly developed form, it is living on cloud nine, losing the sense of time and place. It is total surrender. It is the "sober high."[38]

Professional tennis players speak of playing "in the zone." They take the term from the well-known television show "The Twilight Zone" in which people unexpectedly enter a zone in which they no longer control their lives. Without warning, strange things happen to unsuspecting persons. In tennis, players sometimes enter "the zone" in their match. They have total control over their game without trying to be in control. They play easily and unconsciously to their fullest capacity. It is like playing on a higher plane. Billie Jean King says, "When it happens, I want to stop the match and grab the microphone and shout, 'that's what it's all about!' Because it is. It's just having done something that's totally pure and having experienced the perfect emotion..."[39] Zoning happens in all phases of life. The artist paints in the zone, a dancer dances in it, a musician plays in it, an actor acts in it. And a person can work and live in it. It is the recreative lifestyle attitude condensed, pure and simple. It encompasses the very basic pleasures of a full belly to highly sophisticated intellectual pursuits.

When you live in the recreative lifestyle attitude, you are one with your surroundings. You do not want to make an imprint on the environment or manipulate the world. Instead, you let things come into you and you melt with them. You want to feel, be aware and experience. And that is really the true state of being at ease, being at leisure and having a recreative lifestyle attitude.

37

The Cataclysmic Lifestyle Attitude

Modern life operates almost exclusively in the analytic lifestyle attitude and is not balanced by the recreative one. When you live life in your head, you lose touch with what is going on around and within you. You lose your orientation. It is as though you are in vertigo. You are perplexed and your actions are chaotic. The head, once the pride of man, becomes his downfall. Uneasiness leads to anxiousness, to anxiety, to dread or *Lebensangst* (fear of life). The head no longer is connected to the body. I call this condition the *Cataclysmic Lifestyle Attitude*.

A cataclysm is an overwhelming upheaval, a disaster. When you are ruled by a cataclysmic lifestyle attitude, your life turns into a disaster. Thinking carried to its extreme becomes the carrier of chaotic-perplexed action-awareness patterns. Your awareness is distorted and your actions are disoriented. Life is no longer grounded and a break with reality occurs. This idea has been fittingly expressed as far back as 1763 by the English poet, Charles Churchill:[40]

> With curious Art the Brain too finely wrought
> Preys on herself, and is destroy'd by Thought.
> Constant Attention wears the active mind,
> Blots out her pow'rs, and leaves a blank behind.

The German philosopher, Goethe, called the dangers of getting lost in thought "thinking about thinking." An existence dominated by anxiety as the result of "overthink" pushes man further and further into a timeless past and future. There he loses contact with his world and unknowingly eludes the present. His thoughts about life become overpowering.

I say we take life much too seriously. We let the little "shitties" of life upset us. Instead of just dismissing them as a part of life, we dwell on them. Pretty soon we have five little "shitties," then ten. They pile up. Ironically, it's not the big problems in life that destroy people, but the accumulation of the little "shitties." You think, "I should be doing this, why don't I do that or I could have done this..." The head explodes! Your awareness is totally perplexed. You're confused. You're puzzled. You can't figure life out. You try to find a specific meaning in life, but it's not there.

The analytic lifestyle attitude becomes a cataclysmic one when your head no longer just dominates your body, but is separated from it. You are not together, as the saying goes, but you still try to control everything and everybody, including yourself. Obviously, total control is an impossibility. But as the need for control becomes overpowering, self-expectations and the demands we put on others increase. Nobody, of course, can live up to these expectations. Not even you. So you program yourself for failure. It is an old story that the more you pursue a person, the less of a chance they have to pursue you. The chaser frightens the chased away. If you come on too strong, all he can do is back off. If you interpret his withdrawal as rejection, you might even come on stronger which will cause him to run away even faster. Because you are lost in the labyrinth of your head, you have no idea what is really going on. You experience dis-ease. Your body gets the brunt of your headtrip and you are on the path toward self-destruction. You have moved from an analytic lifestyle attitude into a cataclysmic.

Anyone who has had an unhappy love affair knows the sick feeling. But while you are in the middle of the situation, you are practically lost. Eventually you get both feet on the ground again, open your eyes and ears, and allow yourself to get in touch with the true situation. Your head and your body move in concert again. You become healthy enough to say to yourself, "I don't need this" and you release it. Often the irony is that as you step back, the other person finds the freedom to approach. The wise saying fulfills itself: "You possess most that which you are able to let go."

The story about an unhappy love affair is only a simple and relatively harmless example. The consequences of cataclysmic lifestyle attitudes are much more severe. On a personal level, they can lead to lifelong dread, free-floating rage, catatonic stupor, mental illness or suicide. For a society or mankind as a whole, they can bring senseless wars, holocausts, or nuclear annihilation. Just as an individual can lose touch with himself, whole societies can. They too can lose touch with nature and have their priorities severely distorted. If you live an abortive lifestyle, you may get an ulcer. You literally burn a hole into your stomach. That stomach is *you*. You are burning a hole into your *self*. Likewise, a society controlled by a cataclysmic lifestyle attitude can wipe out plants, animals, and people. It can burn holes, so to speak, into the earth, the ocean, the air—into life. This is why the recent years in the course of civilization have been called the Age of Anxiety. Last year, nearly a billion prescriptions for tranquilizers were written by physicians in the United States. And tranquilizers are just another name for anti-anxiety drugs. More than ever before has man been living in his head, worrying about the future, worrying about the past, and experiencing more and more pressure.

In the cataclysmic lifestyle attitude, a person is overpowered by the apparent demands of life and the opportunities, but not grounded enough to see them in reality. The dread of life becomes real. The demands, self-inflicted or externally imposed, imagined or otherwise, are perceived as real. This is why, for instance, it is so difficult for adolescents to grow up in an affluent society. They see the wealth, the possibilities, the options and potentials. They have all sorts of desires, influences, drives, and also fears about going out there. They worry about who they are, who they will be, what they will do, what is right and what is wrong. The demands, questions and uncertainties become too much. The young person is like an overloaded ciruit. This is why there is such an increase in teenage run-aways and suicide. The individual sees no way out, no alternatives. He is totally overpowered by perceived obligations. The "shoulds," the "oughts," and the "musts." The young person is afraid of being himself, of giving his own life meaning. He is overpowered by internal and external demands.

Another problem of modern people is the bombardment of too many choices and options. There is so much out there. The "coulds," "mights," and "woulds" dominate. This causes the person to live completely in his head and lose touch with his body. He can't take off; he can't transcend. He experiences contactlessness and becomes alienated from himself. Another word for alienation is estrangement. He becomes a stranger to himself. But the fact remains that the more we move into the head, the more we lose touch with ourselves.

Whenever we see too many opportunities, we become perplexed. We don't know what to reach for first. The other day I went into a book store to buy a book to help my teenage son study for the SAT exam. Entering the store, the thought went through my mind, I hope they have something on the SAT in stock. I walked over to the study aids section and to my horror, there were nine shelves filled with paperbacks, hardbacks, thick books, skinny books, computer programs—all on the SAT and (oh no, I'd forgotten he needed) the ACT. I became cataclysmic. Should I buy one of the $8.95 thick ones or a thinner, more condensed volume? Which was better, faster, easier? I opened a few. They all looked alike. I tried to decipher the approaches. What about the one published by the College Entrance Board itself? Would it be more accurate or would a private company offer the *real* test? I was thoroughly confused. Too many choices. I felt like walking out. I decided right then that the $150 spent to enroll my son in the local college course "How to Prepare for the SAT" was money well spent. Let the professor figure it out.

We have to change. Societies have to change. But the nature of change is very paradoxical. You can't change before you know who you are, and before you know who you are, you are you already. Your lifestyle attitude is already deeply grooved and it is very difficult to change. I catch myself many times when I am acting like a complete jackass and I know that I'm being a jackass, but I cannot help myself. I have to finish my act. Of course, the minute I make a jackass out of myself, my wife jumps on me. And what do I do when I get jumped on? I defend myself. Of course I can't change myself when I'm too busy defending myself. To diffuse the situation, my wife and I have chosen the neutral word "flower pot." Whenever one of us is involved in a "jackass routine," the other says, "flower pot." This means "Jackass in progress. Carry on. Will talk later." Then when we're finished and still later when we're able to neutralize ourselves, we deal with it.

139

Just imagine something like this happening in international politics. It is entirely possible as long as the parties involved do not take themselves and their games too "seriously."

I said before that it is the paradoxical nature of change that you cannot really change when you focus on the desired result and as long as the analytic lifestyle attitude remains the dominant way of living. It keeps you preoccupied with who you should be, who you could have been, who you might be if . . ., who your mother wants you to be, etc. The truth is you won't become any of these things before you don't get in touch with who you *are* right this moment. In order to do that, you have to adopt a recreative lifestyle attitude, one that allows you to look at yourself in your present existence. Instead of worrying why you are so upset, you must let yourself feel being upset. My mouth is dry, my shoulders are pulled up. My stomach is tight. I am getting sick . . . What am I doing to myself? Do I want to live this way? What changes do I have to make in my life to remove myself from this dilemma? Herein lies the next challenge. And recreators can play an essential part in it. Recreation professionals can help people on the grass roots level become aware of themselves and recognize their cataclysmic lifestyle attitude. Change won't happen through better health insurance, fancy medical equipment, gadgets, or drugs. It has to happen with the person – with you.

38

Lifestyle Attitude Scale

In the previous chapters, the different types of lifestyle attitudes have been discussed on the basis of evolutionary development, from plants and lower animals to mammals and finally, to man. From this ordered sequence, a phylogenetic scale can be established which is divided into the natural and symbolic realms. The chart on page 143 illustrates the different lifestyle attitudes and their respective action-awareness patterns.

TROPISM

To unify the previously discussed material and get a capsulized view of my lifestyle attitude model, let's review the different lifestyle attitudes.

Beginning at the lower end of the scale is the tropism of the plant world. The lifestyle attitude of plants is governed by expansile-impulsive action awareness patterns. Their way of life is ruled by impelling forces within the cells and the orientation toward or away from specific stimuli. Plants react innately and their expansion and growth is involuntary. The lifestyle attitude of tropism is expressed in the movement form of growth.

Lower animals are similarly dominated by innate impulses and also demonstrate a definite stimulus orientation. This is true not only for the lowest, single-celled forms, but also higher species like spiders, fish, and reptiles. The lifestyle attitude of lower animals is governed by motile-impulsive action-awareness patterns. The hiatus between plants and lower animals is, with a few exceptions, motility. Lower animals have the ability to move, but this movement is rigidly geared toward the achievement of innately established goals. There is no opportunity for variation and there is no play on this level. The integrity of the organism is maintained by the constraint of nature. Motility, or the ability to move, occurs on different levels, from the locomotion of a single cell to the movement of whole organisms. Both tropism and taxis are stimulus oriented and are essentially reactions. Both growth and motility are also represented, of course, within the human scale of lifestyle attitudes.

ANIMATE LIFESTYLE ATTITUDE

The next level on the phylogentic scale is the animate lifestyle attitude, characterized by affective-emotive action-awareness patterns. On this level, stimulus orientation is further developed into object orientation. Higher animals, in other words, relate to the world around them not only impulsively through growth and motility, but also through sensing. This process is controlled by the hedonistic self-regulatory mechanism or the ability to perceive pleasure and pain in relation to an object.

In the animate lifestyle attitude, the organism is still within time, without a sense of self or language. It relates through its senses on an emotional level to the environment. The head is in the service of the body and the organism lives under the constraint of nature. Emotion, together with growth and motility, comprise the natural realm of man, his being lived.

RECREATIVE LIFESTYLE ATTITUDE

The next three lifestyle attitudes are those of the symbolic realm, the living life, and are unique to man. The first level on the scale is the recreative lifestyle attitude. It represents the emergence of the person through the discovery of the self. There is no sense of the self in other animals. Only man knows that he is

LIFESTYLE ATTITUDE SCALE

REALM	ACTION-AWARENESS	LIFESTYLE ATTITUDE
SYMBOLIC "LIVING LIFE"	Chaotic/Perplexed (Failing)	CATACLYSMIC
	Cortical/Rational (Thinking)	ANALYTIC
	Sensuous/Intuitive (Feeling)	RECREATIVE
NATURAL "BEING LIVED"	Affective/Emotive (Sensing)	ANIMATE
	Motile/Impulsive (Moving)	TAXIS
	Expansile/Impulsive (Growing)	TROPISM

him*self*, a separate entity from his environment. Humans go beyond instinct and emotion to what could be called emotional thinking which is, in essence, feeling. This feeling level is characterized by a sensuous-intuitive action-awareness pattern. Man relates subjectively and in the here and now to his environment. He is receptive to his world and allows himself to experience sensuously (through his body) and intuitively (through his head). He is spontaneous and creative and responds with the comfort emotions. On this level, the head and body are in concert. He loses himself in the moment and is without a sense of time. He is totally involved in the process of living.

ANALYTIC LIFESTYLE ATTITUDE

On the next level, man is no longer within time, but rather finds time within himself. He knows that he has a past and a future and with the help of language, he has created his own world, the symbolic realm. Cortical-rational action-awareness patterns lift him into the analytic lifestyle attitude, the level characterized by thinking. In it, man relates objectively to the world. He uses reason. His command over the higher integrative functions allows him to anticipate, reminisce, and intellectualize. He is goal oriented. He controls his own destiny and manipulates his environment. No longer constrained by nature, he is in charge of his own life.

The analytic lifestyle attitude is the level of man's higher achievements. It has made it possible for man to improve the quality of his life by planning for the future and learning from the past. Thinking, however, is a two-edged sword. Many people live their lives almost exclusively in the analytic lifestyle attitude. The head dominates the body. They live in the constant stage of anxiousness or anxiety. Thoughts dominate the body, and the body just reacts. The head is the instigator of all sorts of negative thinking. The crisis emotions like anxiety, fear, and aggression begin to rule man's life. If the analytic attitude is not balanced with the recreative, man's strength and that which lifts him above all other creatures, becomes his downfall.

CATACLYSMIC LIFESTYLE ATTITUDE

When the analytic lifestyle attitude dominates, when the balance does not exist, the onset of the cataclysmic lifestyle attitude commences. Man becomes fascinated with his own power, with his ability to control and manipulate. The head is disconnected from the body. The person is no longer "grounded." The action-awareness patterns are perplexed-chaotic. The crisis emotions take over and the person poisons himself. He suffers from the toxemia of living gone awry. He lives thinking about thinking. He is cataclysmic.

In the cataclysmic lifestyle attitude, man loses touch with nature, with his own nature and that of others. He becomes over-powered by self-perceived demands and choices. He participates in creating his own dis-ease. Because he mislives his life, he is beset with chaotic-perplexed lifestyle patterns which can be exhibited in not only minor neuroses, but in a complete break from reality. He is victimized by the head. The head becomes a source of pain, but the body bears the brunt.

39

Man's Neglected Hemisphere

The central nervous system of man really has three brains, each with its own specific function and purpose. Each brain represents an evolutionary level of development. The oldest brain is the reptilian which is basically dominated by the brain stem. It governs the functions and processes that are best described as innate or impulsive. It regulates basic physiological functions of the organism like blood pressure, hormonal balance, and metabolic processes. It is also programmed, so to speak, by ancient patterns of behavior which have aided the survival and maintenance of the species. Like an in-born, inherited learning device, it lives the animal to hunt, eat, obtain shelter, breed, and mate. The reptilian brain even governs the complex social rites of many species as they instinctively choose leaders, form hierarchies within the pack or herd, and build species-specific nests or webs.

The next evolutionary level of man's brain is the mammalian brain or limbic system which governs the emotions. This brain controls the animate attitude of animals and is responsible for endocrine, somatic-visceral, and emotional functions. It apparently receives messages from the organism's hedonistic self-regulatory mechanism which influences the organism's behaviors. It will, of course, respond to that which is pleasureful or tension-

146

reducing, and will retreat from that which is painful or tension-producing.

The third and highest evolutionary brain and the only truly human brain is the highly developed neocortex which governs rational behavior or thinking. This brain controls all the higher integrative functions which permit man to talk and to read, to reason, to compute mathematically, to create, and to partake in symbolic systems. It allows man to dissect, understand, and control his environment. It gives him control over his present and future and provides insights into his past.

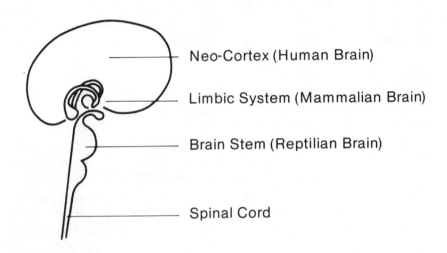

Neo-Cortex (Human Brain)

Limbic System (Mammalian Brain)

Brain Stem (Reptilian Brain)

Spinal Cord

According to MacLean,[41] all three brains are, in essence, separate. Each has its own "biological computer" governing separate functions which are all part of man's inherited "program." Higher animals have a reptilian brain and mammalian brain and even a rudimentary neocortex. But man is the only animal which has such a massive neocortex, which is essentially *the* human brain. MacLean believes the reptilian and mammalian brains to be complementary to each other. They function well together and allow the animal to "be lived" by nature and make primitive decisions to benefit its own nature. A dog knows to eat from the reptilian brain and then it knows what to eat from the mammalian brain. It does not consider how to eat or what time to eat or what to eat tomorrow because it is not equipped to rationalize, having only an incipient neocortex.

Koestler[42] believes the development of the neocortex in humans to be an evolutionary "mistake," an overdevelopment which precludes communication between the emotional brain and the rational brain. It represents a gap between man's emotional life and his thinking life, between emotion and reason. This "schizophysiology" has led to what Koestler calls a "paranoid streak" in human nature.

The concept that there is a gap between the emotions and intellect in human beings is definitely valid, but I feel certain that it is *not* an evolutionary mistake. The gap is due to a cultural misplacement of priorities. And most importantly, man is *not* without the tools to bridge the gap. He has merely chosen, unknowingly, not to use the tools. Much like the shrew who uses his nose to find direction even though he has a perfectly developed sense of sight, man possesses a virtually untapped resource. I am referring to the right side of the brain.

While every human is born with two distinct hemispheres in the neocortex, the left hemisphere is used far more. Left-brain tasks are more valued, encouraged, and rewarded by modern or so-called "advanced" cultures. The consequence is that the right side of the brain of modern man has been neglected. Underused, it is not much more than unrecognized potential. Left-brain thinking has taken over. It has literally conquered the more primitive societies who are more right-brain oriented. Left-brain cultures have perpetuated left-brain dominance by educating its children almost exclusively in left-brain tasks. The two main areas of intellectual endeavor are verbal and mathematical, both of which are left-brain oriented. Very little emphasis is placed on intuition, creativity, or spirituality, which are right-brain endeavors. It is most interesting that the characteristics of the right brain are practically synonymous with the attributes of the recreative lifestyle attitude. And likewise, the characteristics of the left brain are practically synonymous with the attributes of the analytic lifestyle attitude. It is the right hemisphere of the human brain that holds the keys for integrating the emotional and rational natures of man, for bridging the present gap. By uniting the left and right sides of man's neocortex, the analytic lifestyle attitude will be complemented by the recreative lifestyle attitude. Sensing and thinking will be bridged by feeling. Then will man's personhood be complete.

Let's take a closer look at the two hemispheres of the human brain. Man's brain is bicameral. It has two sides, a left and a right. Each hemisphere possesses special powers and governs specific functions. There has been a lot of research into split brain theory and one of the fastest growing areas of brain research concerns cerebral asymmetry or hemispheric dominance. This idea merely suggests that the two hemispheres sometimes act independently from each other and among individuals, one hemisphere can dominate the other. Research dates back to the mid-nineteenth century when Pierre Paul Broca discovered that the center of articulate speech is located in the left frontal cortex. Carl Vernicke also found a sensory speech center in the left hemisphere. It was learned that persons whose left hemisphere was damaged, suffered from speech impairments or aphasia and persons with damaged right hemispheres did not suffer linquistic disturbances, but might suffer difficulties with spatial tasks.

Roger Sperry[43] at the California Institute of Technology did much research on cats. He surgically severed the fibers that connect the hemispheres and studied both sides of the brain. It was discovered that the right hemisphere literally did not know what the left was doing or learning.

It is believed that, in general, right-handed people are governed by the left side of the brain and are "left-brained," and left-handed people are dominated by the right and are "right-brained." Left-handed people comprise about ten to fifteen percent of the population, but only about half of those may be truly biologically left-handed, meaning that their speech centers are in the right hemisphere. If these two hemispheres control different tasks, it is conceivable that right-handed people and left-handed people are really left-brained people and right-brained people who perceive differently and learn differently. It has long been known that among learning-disabled youngsters there is a significantly larger percentage of "lefties."

The chart on page 151 illustrates the functions of the two hemispheres.

It is also interesting how the bicamerality of the human brain relates not only to individuals, but also to whole cultures and to the process of civilization. Julian Jaynes[44] advanced the theory that mankind existed for thousands of centuries without consciousness. He maintains that bicameral civilization evolved from man's acquisition of speech (the left brain) and his inner voices (the right brain) which were attributed to kings and gods. Eventually, due to increasing social complexities, bicameral civilization began to collapse around 2000–1000 BC and man became conscious in the modern sense of the word. Hence, just as the organs and structures of animals change, evolve and adapt, so does the human brain. It also changes and adapts to the demands of its environment and society.

Different cultures stress different values and tasks and, as such, train different centers or hemispheres of the brain. Studies of the Inuit Eskimos[45] reveal a decidedly right hemisphere dominated society. The Inuit people have an incredibly accurate viso-spatial ability and can draw highly complex maps of their territory. Even their language has a spatial right-hemisphere orientation. This obviously shows a high level of adaptability to their Arctic environment. They were observed while creating their well-known native sculptures. They unanimously turned and twisted the creations with their left hand while sculpting with their right. It was as though they used their left hand to obtain a spatial orientation and their right to achieve the details.

European-American society, on the other hand, is highly left-hemisphere oriented. Verbal and mathematical skills are prized and an analytic approach to life far outweighs the artistic, creative, and emotional. The left side of the brain is nurtured in school, at home, and in society at large. They live by the clock, reward logical thinking, symbolic and verbal skills. Even American English is rated by linguistic studies as one of the most analytic of languages.

How does all this tie into Recreation? Recreation is a right-hemisphere process. The recreative lifestyle attitude is receptive. It is a holistic response to life and operates in the here and now. Yet, how can a left-brain dominant society be receptive to such a right-brain attitude? It can't. When Americans, Europeans, or Western people "recreate," they organize left-brain activities and attack them with left-brain vigor and call it play. They organize schedules of activities. They keep score, play competitive sports, and games involving verbal, logical, and mathematical tasks, and thinking. They play or they work in a controlled, detailed, linear, analytic, mechanized world. Western societies view recreation from a left-brainpoint, so to speak. Unfortunately, Western man

150

cannot truly recreate until he can free the other half of his brain and incorporate its talents and strengths into a holistic lifestyle. Western man needs to rediscover his neglected hemisphere and through it, activate his recreative lifestyle attitude.

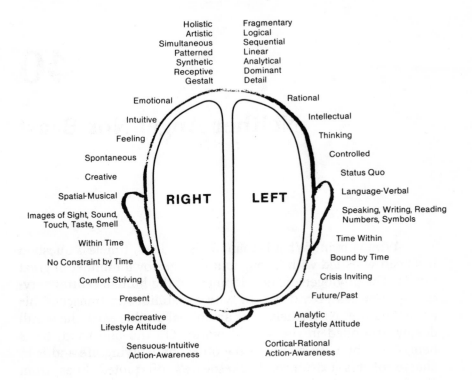

40

Neither Angel Nor Beast

Who is man? What is man? This endless, timeless question has been wrestled with throughout the ages by a number of great minds. The phylogenetic development of the human central nervous system has provided man with capabilities to transcend his animal nature. Nevertheless, as an animal on this earth, he is still deeply grounded in the animal world. On the one hand, he is being lived by nature and on the other, he is living life and is in charge of his existence. Shakespeare's oft-quoted lines from *Hamlet* express joyful pride in the human condition:

> What a piece of work is man! how noble in reason! how infinite in faculty! in form and moving how express and admirable! in action how like an angel! in apprehension how like a god![46]

Writing at the height of the Renaissance period in Italy, Pico della Mirandola[47] also expressed a lofty, optimistic view in his "The Dignity of Man" written in 1486. In it, he says that God, the Architect, formed man as a "creature of undetermined nature" and placed him "in the middle of the universe":

> I created thee a being neither heavenly nor earthly, neither mortal nor immortal only, that thou mightest be free to

shape and to overcome thyself. Thou mayst sink into a beast, and be born anew to the divine likeness. The brutes bring from their mother's body what they will carry with them as long as they live. . . To thee alone is given a growth and a development depending on thine own free will. Thou bearest in thee the germs of a universal life."

When Mirandola refers to brutes bringing "from their mother's body what they will carry with them as long as they live," he really expresses the qualities of the animate lifestyle attitude. Brutes or animals cannot escape the constraint of nature. They are only being lived and this is the limitation of their natural condition. Man, however, is neither heavenly nor earthly but is "given a growth and development depending on thine own free will." In this respect, man is not limited to the animate lifestyle attitude, although he certainly possesses the limbic system and many accompanying characteristics, like emotion. He is free to shape and overcome himself. He has, unlike any other life form, both an analytic and a recreative lifestyle potential. He bears "the germs of a universal life" or the ability to live in perfect harmony within himself and the world around him. Man is neither angel nor beast. He is human. He is responsible for his own destiny. Will he be able to meet the challenge?

Leonardo da Vinci,[48] writing at the same time as Mirandola didn't think so. At the end of his life he offered a much more pessimistic outlook when he wrote "Of the Cruelty of Man":

Creatures shall be seen upon the earth who will always be fighting one with another with very great losses and frequent deaths on either side. These shall set no bounds to their malice; by their fierce limbs a great number of the trees in the immense forests of the world shall be laid level with the ground; and when they have crammed themselves with food it shall gratify their desire to deal out death, affliction, labors, terrors, and banishment to every living thing. And by reason of their boundless pride they shall wish to rise towards heaven, but the excessive weight of their limbs shall hold them down. There shall be nothing remaining on the earth or under the earth or in the waters that shall not be pursued and molested and destroyed, and that which is in one country taken away to another; and their own bodies shall be made the tomb and the means of transit of all the living bodies which they have slain. O Earth! which delays thee to open and hurl them headlong into the deep fissures of thy huge abysses and caverns, and no longer to display in the sight of heaven so savage and ruthless a monster?

The views of men are shaped by the circumstances under which they live. Da Vinci was the product of the wealthy merchant class of Florence which at the time was ruled by the brutal power of the notorious Sforza and Borgia families. Influenced by the court of these people, he was encouraged to design all sorts of machines of war. Having witnessed and indirectly been a party to death and destruction, his writings reflect an excess of pessimism and despair.

But, is his description of man not representative of the cataclysmic lifestyle attitude? "They shall wish to rise toward heaven, but the excessive weight of their own limbs shall hold them down." The head is separated from the body. Da Vinci maintains that man has taken the task of fashioning himself and developed all forms of human aggression, particularly greed, violence, and cruelty. In one respect this may be true. That these aggressions are essentially human manifestations and do not exist in the animal world is a valid observation. They definitely are not the byproduct of man's animalistic nature. They are a human product and the result of ineptness, of social and cultural dis-ease and a cataclysmic lifestyle attitude. Since this lifestyle attitude and its accompanying disaster represents the biggest threat to the continuance of civilization, let's examine the concept of aggression and man's role concerning it.

Recent literature (Lorenz et al.)[49] suggests that aggression is an innate drive which has its roots in the animal world or as I would call it, in the natural realm. This hypothesis grants a justification for man's aggression. On the basis of this theory, man is considered bad *by nature*. He cannot help himself but be aggressive and therefore must learn to sublimate his aggressive drives, those with which he has been born. This concept of sublimation has become one of the main goals of people in the helping professions, from psychiatrists to priests.

I personally believe that human aggression is largely the result of socialization. It is the result of distress, the frustration of unfulfilled drives, or of lifestyle patterns that promote aggressive

154

behavior. Observations in nature show no really innate aggression, but only conditions that bring about aggressiveness. The life of an animal is controlled by drives for sex, hunger, protection of territory, and self-preservation. The animal is still being lived and driven to activities. I would say that the animal world is ruled by *activity drives,* but aggression as such is only the result of lifestyle conditions that result from the animal's innate striving for a steady state, for satisfaction. In nature there is no aggression, only conditions that instigate aggressiveness. If the drives are not satisfied, frustration and pain arise and then nature attempts to satisfy the frustration. The aggression drive is not genetically transmitted or inherited. It is created by conditions in the environment. Man, in other words, has the ability to create conditions that would allow him to satisfy his basic needs. So the theory of innate aggression is really a myth. It is an easy way out for man to excuse greed, violence, and cruelty. The mistake that initiated this misconception is that the animal's natural life state is translated in anthropomorphic terms. That is, human characteristics are ascribed to non-human objects (in this case, animals) and then conclusions are drawn from these perceptions. These misperceptions are then reapplied to explain animal behavior.

In the case of aggression, all animals exhibit aggressiveness in the fulfillment of their needs. It is merely the mode with which humans observe and evaluate the aggressiveness that promotes misunderstanding. For instance, if a lion leaps on a young gazelle, throws it on its back and savagely disembowels it, we would observe that as violent aggression. When a horse tears alfalfa from its bale and chomps hungrily, we would not associate it so readily with aggression. And surely when a hummingbird robs a hibiscus blossom of its nectar, we definitely would not associate it with aggression. Yet, all of these behaviors are the same. The animal in its own way is demonstrating *aggressiveness,* which is the mode of activity with which basic needs are satsfied and tension is reduced. The animal is definitely not demonstrating *aggression.* There is no unnecessary violence, no blood lust, no intentional cruelty, and no greed. A lion wrongfully is termed "king of the jungle" in the sense that it does not collect and hoard the corpses of gazelles, nor does it seek power and dominance over animals outside his own species.

Aggression, that is, intentional cruelty, violence and greed, is a human phenomenon and the result of ineptness and dis-ease. In

155

my opinion, it is rooted in lifestyle attitude patterns which promote crisis emotions. It originates in the symbolic realm and is a product of culture. The famous Protestant theologian, Calvin, [50] wrote "men are vicious by nature." More fitting might be, *men are aggressive by culture.* According to Gay,[51] "Men are bloodthirsty, superstitious, prejudiced and xenophobic. Human history is full of oppression, intolerance, calculated exploitation, and gratuitous atrocity. Governments are callous and tyrannical, public opinion fickle, credulous and cruel; customs and institutions by which men live and to which they often fanatically cling contain so much brutality and absurdity."

Still, I think that the question of where man's aggression originates is really of secondary importance. There is no doubt that human aggression is greatly dictated by environmental conditions. The emphasis should be put on ways that societies can reduce aggression. Lorenz praises the value of sports in the sublimation of aggression. But sublimation is nothing more than the replacement of socially unacceptable, tension-reducing behavior with acceptable. And although the technique of expression is different, the underlying attitude is not changed. Aggression in sports can build readiness for killing in an acceptable way. Pre-military education programs of highly nationalistic countries always give sports a high priority. It is the tool for political indoctrination and preparation for war with the goal being the destruction of the enemy. In order to eliminate aggression in sports, the emphasis should be on instilling positive aggressiveness in athletes to play the sport to their highest capability. They should aggressively run, hit, kick, pass, throw, and pursue the ball to their best ability. They should aggressively pursue individual excellence and team cooperation. They should not destroy, hurt, wipe-out, cream, or kill the other team. They are not engaged in aggressive competition, only in athletic excellence. They are pursuing cooperation aggressively, not aggression competitively.

It is a change in attitude that must be carried into all aspects of human life. In the business world, merchant values are deeply rooted in aggression. The emphasis is not on aggressively producing a better product. It is on destroying or eliminating the opposition. Advertising campaigns of food and soft drink companies based on attacking the competition proliferate. Ethically, they hit each other "below the belt." And needless to say, politics, from a local to a global level, is the champion in the arena of aggression.

Aggression, then, is dependent on the prevailing lifestyle attitude. Before man can strive for peace, he must strive for self-satisfaction or appeasement. Only this way can he avoid inner discord and be at ease. When we are at ease, we are at peace with ourselves. And when we are at peace with ourselves, we are at peace with others. The responsibility for this process always returns to the individual who must learn to live at ease, with himself and the world around him.

41

Illness, Ineptness and Dis-Ease

When we say a person is ill, we immediately assume that he is the victim of a particular disease. And when you're a victim, you are helpless. You can't do anything about it. You need someone else to help you. You need an expert to make you healthy again. Of course, if you are born with a certain illness, or predisposition for it, or if you contract a contagious disease or virus, then you are indeed helpless. You caught it or it caught you. You surely did not take any part in contracting it.

The traditional concept of illness belongs in the natural realm of life, in which maladies are caused by germs, viruses, genetic imperfection, or traumatic accident. In this view, man becomes sick by nature or by an act of God. It belongs into the "being lived" part of the lifestream because you are indeed a victim of life's circumstances. You are helpless. *Que sera, sera,* as the Spanish saying goes. If you are born with malformed limbs or with a limited intellectual capacity, you are helpless with regard to your condition. In the same manner, disabling things can happen to you at times during your life. You could be innocently walking on the sidewalk and a car runs into you and you lose both legs. In such a case, although there was interference from other people, there was still a high degree of helplessness in your plight. It happened to you. In the case of poliomyelitis, the virus infiltrates your central nervous system and causes damage. Once the acute stage is over, you are left with paralysis or crippled limbs. You were just unlucky to have been at the wrong place at the wrong time.

But many illnesses are of a different kind. They are the type in which the person actively participates in his illness and belong in the "living life" realm of the lifestream. I am thinking specifically of those often referred to as psychosomatic disorders which are the direct reflection of a person's abortive lifestyle. The person participates in his disorder by living life in disharmony and thereby exposing himself to self-created dis-ease. Simple examples are smoking too much, drinking too much, overeating, or "burning the candle at both ends." Equally destructive are the types of dis-ease caused by too much thinking. These can range from general worrying to "losing one's mind" and escaping reality altogether. Other common disorders of this sort include not only migraines, peptic ulcers, high blood pressure, respiratory ailments, but also possibly some types of cancer, and, in my opinion, the majority of so-called mental illnesses.

I do not like to think of these complaints as genuine illnesses in which you are either born with a condition or later in life contract a physical disability. For those disorders you are an active participant. I prefer to use the term dis-ease when referring to something you do to yourself. You bring about dis-ease.

Many of the dis-eases that are of a participatory nature are actually the healthy reaction of the organism to an unhealthy lifestyle. A migraine, an ulcer, depression, or whatever are warning signals from the body. It is healthy for the body to scream, "Stop living like this. You're killing me!" But we don't get the message. We continue living the same way, swallowing pills to hide the symptoms, repairing ulcerated stomach linings through surgery, and at best altering a single lifestyle pattern such as diet or exercise.

Of course, the question remains, which came first, the chicken or the egg? Do changes in blood flow patterns or in the electrochemical processes of the brain cause mental illness or are these changes the direct result of ineptness, that is, a cataclysmic lifestyle attitude? I'm convinced that in the vast majority of cases, the symptoms are rooted in the person's way of life. Their origins are in the symbolic realm, not the natural one. Definitely, mental illness is not a drug deficiency and psychopharmacological treat-

159

ment is not a solution. It treats symptoms only and as such is a cover-up. The solution lies within the individual and his culture.

Our tendency is to explain bizarre or deviant behavior by examining the body for physical or chemical causes. In the San Ysidro massacre, the slain killer was given an autopsy in which brain tissue was examined for abnormalities. None were found. The solution for problems in living is not found in man's nature, but in himself and in the way he lives his life.

It is erroneous and outright dangerous to include dis-ease under the traditional medical model of illness and thereby remove the responsibility of the individual's participation from the process. The ability to respond is taken away from the individual and handed over to methods of intervention by the expert. The part that the person plays in his own dis-ease becomes obscured. He is given the impression that he is victimized by illness when in fact he is, in varying degrees, directly responsible for his condition. He hands himself and his problem to the expert who treats his symptoms only.

When the organism is overworked and needs rest, it may break down by contracting a cold or feeling sluggish and fatigued. Bad environmental conditions ranging from poisoned air to junk food also have the organism sending out distress signals. The last thing that is needed are treatment modalities. An overworked body certainly doesn't need an amphetamine to keep it going and counteract the feelings of fatigue. Nor does it need a cold tablet to take away the symptoms of headache and congestion. What is desperately needed is a change in the lifestyle. Slow down! A car with an overheated engine is pulled over and cooled off. We treat our cars better than our bodies.

The majority of illnesses in this world belong into this category of dis-ease. They are the result of living in the cataclysmic lifestyle attitude. This may be out of ignorance, fanaticism, immaturity or downright stupidity. Szasz[52] refers to these disorders as problems in living. I like the word "ineptness" as a collective term.

Man can, up to a certain point, escape the constraint of nature and become responsible for his own life. Often, however, he demonstrates a lack of understanding for setting his own limitations. He doesn't know when he has had enough. He has a history of overdoing everything. He overeats, overdrinks, overruns, overpowers, and most destructively, overthinks.

Too much of anything, even if it seems good for you, will eventually work against you. Even preoccupation with your health can lead to anything from digestive disorders to hypochondriasis or anorexia nervosa. Such "dis-eases" originate not with a bacteria or virus, that is, in the natural realm, but within the overactive human neocortex, which is representative of the symbolic realm.

A healthy lifestyle attitude is the harmonious mingling of the natural and symbolic realms. Harmony brings health. Disharmony, resulting from ineptness, brings free-floating anxiety or aggression, or even self-destruction. The suffering from this ineptness is real, but the sufferer is not really ill. Unable to escape his analytic lifestyle attitude, he is unable to tune into himself and the world around him. He becomes cataclysmic. He is inept.

Most illness is really dis-ease and does not have its origin in the natural realm but in the symbolic realm. The dis-ease symptoms of an organism are only "natural" reactions to an abortive lifestyle caused by ineptness—not knowing how to live. Szasz suggests "that the phenomena now called mental illnesses...be removed from the category of illnesses, and that they be regarded as the expressions of man's struggle with the problem of *how* he should live."[53]

There are varying degrees of participation in illness. Functional mental disorders are of a highly participatory variety. And it is a great mistake to put them into the hands of the medical profession. They are much more related to values and ethics, and should be handled as issues of everyday living, rather than treated as illnesses. The diagram below illustrates the varying degrees of participation from illness to ineptness.

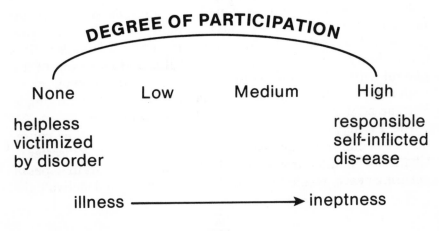

DEGREE OF PARTICIPATION

| None | Low | Medium | High |

helpless
victimized
by disorder

responsible
self-inflicted
dis-ease

illness ——————→ ineptness

Many intelligent people lead inept, stupid lives. Both healthy, with the capacity to enjoy life to the fullest, they live bored, apathetic, anxious, self-defeated, guilty, and unzestful existences. Their ineptness promotes organismic deterioration. Unable to find meaning or hope in life, they become neurotic. As Maslow[54] expresses it "giving gratification to neurotic needs does not breed health as does gratification of basic inherent needs. Giving a neurotic power-seeker all the power he wants does not make him less neurotic, nor is it possible to satiate his neurotic need for power. However much he is fed, he still remains hungry."

This stupidity about life is ineptness. I fully believe that so-called mental illness is initiated to a great extent by the person himself. He is overpowered by self-manufactured demands and too many choices. By necessity, in order to survive, and therefore, healthily, he designs a lifestyle in which he can cope. He gets depressed; he withdraws. He makes himself psychotic or schizophrenic. But he survives! The label "schizophrenia" is interesting because "schizo" comes from the Greek meaning "split" and "phrenum" is from the same root as the word "diaphragm" which is the middle of the torso. Schizophrenics are truly split in half. They are cut in two at the chest. Their head is not in contact with the body. They live strictly in the head.

Mental illness is nothing more than ineptness, the inability to recognize life for what it is. And just as the individual can participate in the creation of his own ineptness, he also can participate in the process of liberation—freeing himself from the shackles of the cataclysmic lifestyle attitude.

What is true about individuals is true about whole cultures. Collective neuroses, aggressions, depressions, frustrations all lead to epidemics, wars, pollutions, fanaticism, etc. Dis-eased societies become inept and exhibit a mass "stupidity about life." To paraphrase Calvin again, we might say *men are stupid by culture*. It is our inability to recognize life for what it is and make out of it a playful experience, not taking it too gravely, but flowing along with nature within the bounds of nature. We toil at life, trying to become masters of life and eventually, we fail at life.

The TV movie "Special Bulletin" illustrates the extreme consequence of cultural ineptness. It was the story of nuclear disaster in Charleston, South Carolina. In this story, five scientists in hopes of ensuring peace, wanted to force the government to deactivate the

953 stockpiled missiles. They built a nuclear bomb and master-minded a scheme to coerce the government into submission. The government overtly complied, but secretly staged a counterattack. Using a tugboat, the government men boarded the warship where the detonation ritual was to take place. In the course of the action, four of the scientists were killed and one taken prisoner. The atomic bomb needed to be defused, but it had been double-rigged. It had so many computerized feedbacks, it was impossible to dismantle it. As the last seconds ticked by, it became evident that the dreadful explosion would occur. It happened. The mushroom cloud rose in the background. Many characters you had been following for nearly two hours died instantly. The announcer that was covering the story from an aircraft carrier two miles away uttered her last words knowing that within five minutes the radiation would reach her and she would die. All the persons involved were either dead or traumatized and dying. This is the ultimate global ineptness. Being so *stupid* over an issue to destroy oneself. The station received many phone calls from confused or upset viewers even though it flashed constant announcements that the show was a dramatization. In some ways it was like the famous 1938 broadcast, "War of the Worlds," but with one overwhelming difference. In 1983 we were not being invaded by otherworldly aggressors. We were not the helpless, innocent victims. In "Special Bulletin," we were the inept participants in our own dis-ease and destruction.

Human beings all have the ability, the power and the responsibility to alter the course of themselves and their cultures. Being at leisure is not only a pleasant lifestyle attitude, it is an urgent necessity. For civilization to progress, for culture to bloom and for the arts to flourish, man must actively participate in overcoming his self-created ineptness and dis-ease.

42

Preventive Medicine at Its Best

Within the framework of Western tradition, it is common practice to confront a situation directly and if there is resistance, to fight it. As in the sport of boxing, power is met with power, and the antagonistic position is maintained to the knock-out. In contrast to boxing are the martial arts like Judo, Karate, Kung Fu, and Tai Chi. These sports, originating in the Orient, reflect the Eastern way of thinking. In these sports, you go with the power of your opponent. You tune into the flow of his energy and use it to bring closure to a threatening situation.

In much the same way, Western medicine reflects Western thought. Illness is attacked with treatment and more treatment. For example, stomach ulcers are treated surgically and portions of the stomach are routinely removed. The causes for the ulcer may not be addressed, and the same unhealthy lifestyle may be pursued. If nervous tension and pent-up emotions are the cause, perhaps drugs, or at best, a different dietary plan may be prescribed. The ulcer has been attacked and removed, but the problem lifestyle which caused it remains intact. Such surgical, drug, anti-disease oriented thinking has long pervaded traditional American medicine and only recently have other approaches like holistic healing, and preventive medicine become even remotely acceptable.

By moving *with* that which is healthy, the energies of a person are activated in a movement toward health. Recreation is moving with health. Health is promoted through active participation. And the participatory role of the person is central to the process of recreation. Disease is indirectly affected by moving with health. How different this is from going *against* disease.

Several years ago I spoke to the staff of the Recreation Center for the Handicapped in San Francisco about the principle of moving with a situation instead of going against it. A couple of weeks after my presentation, a young worker at the Center named Oliver who had heard me speak visited me and said:

> Bruno, I have to share a story with you. You won't believe what happened. I heard your talk about moving with instead of going against something. Well, we have a boy at the Center who crawls underneath a table and hides whenever it is time to leave for an outside activity. I always have to drag him out while he kicks and screams and the whole thing turns into a horror show. But last time when he disappeared under the table, I crawled in after him. At first he looked startled and began to run away on all fours. I followed him all around the room on my hands and knees and then, suddenly, I turned and began to run away from him. He began chasing me as I ran down the hall and into the waiting van. He was right behind me, laughing and having a great time as he unknowingly boarded the van. Moving with an originally awkward situation did the trick.

Now this does not mean that Oliver discovered a new "van-loading technique." Chances are, the next time or with another person, this might not work. I stress this point because I have met so many professionals and students in the helping professions who are forever seeking "techniques." This is dangerous. Their concern is not with people, but with their own needs in handling people. They seem to think the answer is in discovering the right technique. A perfect example is the "primal scream"[55] therapy which became fashionable in the early seventies. For a lot of people, the ability to scream brought great relief to them. But to make a "technique" out of screaming destroyed the very essence of its therapeutic value. As soon as you know in advance that screaming is good for you or that screaming is the goal, you keep yourself from ever screaming spontaneously. By establishing a preconceived goal, you provide an artificial basis for doing something you don't really feel like doing. You end up going against yourself and thereby keeping yourself from genuinely experiencing what might have happened otherwise. You might even end up hurting rather than helping yourself.

Going with a seemingly antagonistic or dangerous situation can be well illustrated through a movement example like ski racing. If a downhill skier is going sixty miles an hour on ice and his skis catch an edge, he must make a split-second decision: Do I try to recover or do I go with the fall? If his decision to recover comes too late, the fall will take over and pull him apart. This is when the big "egg beaters" happen. Downhillers don't survive too many of those without serious injury. If, on the other hand, he decides still early enough to go with the fall, he will be able to maintain some control, pull up his knees and avoid getting hurt. A downhill racer quits when he can no longer make this decision at the right time. In order to avoid serious injury, he must not fight the fall, but go with it. He must allow himself to fall with the momentum, with nature. And by surrendering to the fall, to the forces of nature, he takes the more risk-free solution and keeps himself from getting seriously hurt.

Modern man, unfortunately, still tries to control or attack life. In the process he loses touch with nature and creates the big "egg beaters" of living which are the products of his dis-ease. They range from psychosomatic disorders to mental illness, from air pollution to acid rain, from toxic waste dumps to nuclear disaster, from religious to political wars.

As long as man's way of life remained in harmony with nature's way, his existence was protected by it. He lived under the constraint of nature. This is no longer the case. Man has taken life more and more into his own hands. He has saturated his life with symbolic meaning. Obsessed by the need to control, he has upset the delicate balance of nature. As a result, *Being Lived* and *Living Life* do not flow harmoniously. The balanced flow of the life-stream is disrupted. Customs, confusions and an accelerated pace all remove man more and more from the natural way. Out of the resulting disharmony, conflict and dis-ease arise.

166

Recreation does not go against dis-ease; it moves with health. Recreation promotes the change from a cataclysmic to a recreative lifestyle attitude. Recreation moves toward a harmonious relationship with nature. Recreation is applied preventive medicine at its best.

43

Systems Theory and Recreation

The most perplexing problem I encounterd after my first year as a student at the University of Vienna was the limitations created by the fragmentation of general knowledge into narrow academic disciplines. My main interest was quite simply – people. I wanted to find out "what makes people tick?" But the answers I sought were not readily available in any of the isolated disciplines like sociology, biology, or psychology. The individual courses did not relate to each other. There was no synthesis.

Fortunately I was permitted to cross departmental lines and design my own program. I took courses in physiology, movement education, existentialism, philosophy of science, ethics, physical therapy, clinical psychology, etc. The more I studied, the more I became convinced of the indivisible wholeness of the human organism and its interdependence with other organisms and their social and natural environments.

One day as I went to meet a friend after his philosophy class, I fell into a lecture in which the professor was introducing a new idea which he called an "organismic concept." It was based on the premise that organisms are not mere conglomerations of separate elements, but "systems" exhibiting wholeness, organization, and constant flux. *"Der Organismus aehnelt eher einer Flamme als einem*

Kristall oder Atom" were his very words. (The organism resembles a flame rather than a crystal or an atom.) I followed his lecture with interest and was excited to have found what I had been looking for, substantiation for my belief that all the complexities of life are interrelated.

Only at the very end of the lecture did I suddenly realize who the professor was. When I was a junior in the classical secondary school, I had visited his home as a friend of his son. I remember seeing the professor behind a large desk surrounded by books. Little did I realize then that Dr. Ludwig von Bertalanffy,[56] the founder of General Systems Theory, would become such a major influence on my own thinking.

Since that first lecture at the Philosophical Faculty, I have followed the writings and the developments of systems research. I have become a member of the Society for General Systems Research and serve as papers referee in leisure sciences for the new journal, *Systems Research.*

I wholeheartedly believe the systems approach is the ideal perspective for the field of leisure sciences and recreation. The field encompasses a broad spectrum of subject matter which reaches far beyond those associated with established disciplines or professions. For this very reason, the field has traditionally lacked cohesion from within, as well as acceptance by the scientific community. Recreators have long realized that there is an urgent need for new ways of looking at the world. Adjectives like holistic, ecological, synergistic, organismic and global have long been an essential part of their vocabulary. Man is simply not separate from this world. He is a system, made up of systems, and living within systems. The General Systems approach can serve as a link between recreation and leisure sciences and other fields of human endeavor.

What exactly is systems theory? Bertalanffy originated the term "General Systems Theory."[57] He defined it as "the formulation and derivation of those principles which are valid for 'systems' in general." GST might be considered a science of "wholeness." Together with Rapaport, Boulding, and Gerard, he founded the Society for General Systems Research in 1954 in Palo Alto, California. In their writings they stressed the fact that both material systems such as social institutions, countries, and organisms, and non-material ones such as language and music qualify as systems. Each of these systems acts as a whole and is interrelated with other systems. This is why GST is considered to be a holistic science. Followers of systems theory consider man himself to be an open and active system. For Rapaport,[58] a system is a portion of the world that is perceived as a unit and is able to maintain its "identity" in spite of changes occurring in it. Of course, man is such a unit. He changes from within and from without. He has spontaneity. Man is not just reactive or passive. He is creative. He participates spontaneously in life. According to Maslow,[59] spontaneity is the essence of self-actualization which is built upon Bertalanffy's "spontaneous goal-seeking activity" of every organism. Humanness, then, has biological roots.

General Systems Theory had its origin in organismic biology, but has found its way into practically all fields of human endeavor. Modern technology has adopted the systems approach in the control and organization of research, industry, defense, transportation and communications. Ecology has long recognized the wholeness of man and his environment and has applied systems ideas. Likewise, in the areas of management and computer science, systems theory prevails. And the list goes on. The applications of GST abound in the life and human sciences, including medicine, mental health, psychology, sociology, linguistics, political science, and the humanities. Of course, recreation and the leisure sciences have long integrated the subject matter of these hereto divergent fields. GST offers a methodological reorientation and interdisciplinary cross-fertilization in the understanding of life on earth and the wholeness of nature.

Laszlo[60] begins his book, *An Introduction to Systems Philosophy*, by asking for a return from analytic to synthetic philosophy. He urges that we overcome our "patchwork approach" to problems of living and recognize that we are a part of an interconnected system of nature. He calls for "informed generalists" to make it their business to develop systemic theories of the patterns of interconnection." Recreators *are* such generalists. They are aware of the holistic nature of individuals, groups, and environments.

The future implications of systems approach are recognized by respected thinkers in many fields of learning. The general consensus is that a wider observational approach must be taken in order to make the affairs of human existence better understood. As Laszlo further writes, ". . . our short-range projects and limited

170

controllabilities may lead us to our own destruction." The social scientist, Martin Shubik[61] states, "We need knowledge, insight and breadth of view." The political scientist, Herbert Spiro,[62] considers systems theory indispensable to all areas of political science. Tinbergen,[63] the biologist, stresses the need to understand "the whole system of phenomena in order to see each individual problem in its perspective." The task is overwhelming, but the urgency for change is only too apparent.

The responsibility for changes in lifestyle attitude must come from the individual. You have to be "able to respond." By our very existence, you and I participate in the greater things of life. This is the reason why science and human values cannot be separated. Science exists to promote human values through technological progress. But technological progress cannot promote human values. Who can? Only people can. By their lifestyle attitude. By the way they live. And living goes far beyond people. It reaches into everything they come in contact with. It was Winston Churchill[64] who once said, "First we shape our buildings and then our buildings shape us." Houses reflect the lifestyle attitudes of the people who occupy them. Instant slums breed slum people who in turn breed more slums. Systems within systems within systems.

The philosopher, Camus,[65] insists that "each society has the criminals it deserves." Somehow we all participate in the formation of the milieu that surrounds us, through the objects we use and the values we cherish and by the way you and I live our lives. The input of each person is very important. But we pay little attention to the power of the individual. Instead we center our energies on external aspects of life. This peripheral fragmentation is causing disunity and alienation. We lose touch with our collective consciousness, with our global lifestyle attitude, with the way we *are* on this earth. We have to raise our consciousness, increase our wisdom and grow up to become truly human. If I look around in the world today, I realize that technologically we are living in the Space Age, but emotionally we haven't come further than the Stone Age. For us, in order to survive, our wisdom will have to catch up with our knowledge. Otherwise, our increase in knowledge will only increase our dilemma. In the words of the great novelist and poet, Hermann Hesse, "The true profession of man is: To find his way to himself."

171

44

Playing At Life

   Most people genuinely believe that human labor, the daily job, their career is the core of their life, and such cultural beliefs are passed on to the young, and perpetuated by educational systems which are still job and career oriented. Schools are still disseminating fact upon fact about jobs and careers which will soon no longer exist. Most young people today subscribe whole-heartedly to the idea that they must orient themselves to a career and spend the next forty years of their adult lives pursuing that career. And ironically, because of the imposed system by which we live which offers no alternative except "societal dependence" like welfare and other degrading subsidies, indeed they must pursue outdated goals. They must give up living today in order to have, to do, to be later.

   At the present, man lives in a technological world which is end-product oriented. He has created this world through endless work and diligence. He has repressed his natural yearning to play and to enjoy in the process, and this may well lead to the most significant crisis in his survival. I foresee a not-so-distant day when it will dawn on people like an idea whose time has come that the values we have held for so long are no longer applicable. Natural and artificial scarcities are contrived, human toil is extraneous to survival,

172

and crisis emotions are a sorry means of motivation. And then will come the greatest social revolution that civilization has ever fathomed.

We must create a culture that approves the sensual and permits the playful. The present direction of man's emotions is crisis-oriented. We act out of fear, or out of aggression. The cold war, the arms escalation, the mutual distrust of political systems and ideologies are all manifestations of fear and aggression. And they are crisis-bound. It is only too evident that the technology which could free man, could also be the source of his destruction and the total annihilation of life on earth.

The German philosopher, Friedrich Nietzsche,[66] predicted the isolated period of "nihilism" which would come when man is unable to adapt, cope with or understand the full implications of his self-created technocracy. He visualized a time when man would be too shocked by the benevolent upheaval caused by science and technology to deal with it or appreciate it. After the initial disorientation, however, man would come to understand the new environment and live with it, not against it. Then, for the first time in the history of civilization, there would exist a global society in which the environment would aid and support mankind. In such a society, the dualism of work and play will no longer exist. Play will be the central theme of human living, rather than a frivolous part-time escape. It will become the sphere of creativity and spontaneity, of aesthetic pursuits, and the development of all that is civilization. The "Age of Aquarius" will have then truly dawned.

The eminent biologist and Pulitzer Prize-winning author, Rene Dubos,[67] was commissioned by the Secretary General of the United Nations Conference of the Human Environment in May 1971 to chair a committee of scientific and intellectual leaders from 58 countries. On the basis of the results of this committee and his own observations, Dubos listed in his book, *The Wooing of the Earth,* the major dangers that threaten humankind and the earth. The list, in order of importance was:

1. Nuclear warfare
2. Failure to provide meaningful employment for young people
3. Overpopulation
4. Environmental degradation

5. Excessive use of energy and resources

6. Environmental pollution

Of major significance is the number 2 concern, "failure to provide meaningful employment for young people." This situation
does not apply merely to lack of jobs. It goes much deeper into
feelings of meaninglessness, inadequacy, and ultimately dehu-
manization and desocialization. Never before have I seen this
concern given such a high priority. I am in full agreement, however. This problem leads to a mass ineptness and consequently to
a cataclysmic lifestyle attitude. It is, in my opinion, the most
critical problem facing mankind today. If the world cannot change
from the classical work ethic which is linked with toil and anxiety
to a leisure ethic which is associated with fulfillment and joy, then
the tender bomb within might go off earlier and more devastatingly
than the nuclear one.

We need new ways of thinking, followed up by new ways of living. In other words, we need to change the prevailing lifestyle attitudes. Our present world is guided by the analytic lifestyle attitude which is dominated by the crisis emotions and all too often
enters the cataclysmic sphere. We are still ruled by disconnected
thought. We fragment and isolate. Not only do we disconnect our
head from our body and the mental from the physical, we separate
ourselves from others and culture from nature. The theoretical
physicist, David Bohm,[68] wrote:

> The widespread distinctions between people (race, nation,
> etc.) which are now preventing mankind from working
> together...for survival (are largely caused by) the kind of
> thought that treats things as inherently...disconnected.
> So what is needed is for man to give attention to his habit
> of fragmentary thought, to be aware of it, and thus to bring
> it to an end.

We are also the victims of excessive thought. We think too
much. Overthink can lead, among other things, to overkill. Each
U.S. Poseidon submarine[69] can deliver the explosive force of 500
times that of the Hiroshima bomb. That is twice as much fire
power as all the munitions used in World War II in which nearly
50 million people were killed. And that is only *one* submarine, one
small fraction of the total destructive force of all the superpowers
on earth. Translate the results of all the human effort and mone-

tary expenditure used to manufacture and maintain such an arsenal into cooperative efforts. What kind of a world would it be? As H. G. Wells[70] warned in the years prior to World War II, civilization was losing "the race between education and catastrophe."

We need to educate for leisure. Modern man does not know what leisure is. He is hypnotized by an outmoded Zeitgeist. He has to be dehypnotized through consciousness-raising, a process which operates on three levels. First of all, he must intellectually grasp the concept of leisure. Secondly, he must recognize the importance of the concept and be able to apply it. And thirdly, he must incorporate the concept into his lifestyle attitude by living it.

In the days of Ancient Greece, Plato[71] said, "the unexamined life is not worth living." He stressed the importance of knowledge for its own sake as a chief ingredient of the good life. Later, during the Industrial Revolution with its glorification of work, the phrase changed to "the unproductive life is not worth living." In other words, labor and utility became the focal point. The question that man asked himself changed from "what shall I know?" to "what shall I do?" The question now and for the future is "how shall I live?" guided by the insight that only the sagacious life is worth living. Wisdom, then, is the ultimate goal.

The by-product of wisdom is cooperation instead of competition, comfort rather than crisis, and play rather than toil. Ineptness, disease and drudgery lead to an existence marred by toiling at life and eventually by failing at life. As the deceptively simple Buddhist saying goes, "Only happy people can make a happy world." Dubos[72] advances the idea that "the most useful citizens are not necessarily those who increase production and knowledge, but rather those who generate *joie de vivre* around them." Only a life deeply rooted in the recreative lifestyle attitude will bring meaning, fulfillment, and joy to working, learning, and living.

Being at leisure is playing at life.

References

PART I

1 Adler, Mortimer J. *Liberal Education.* Industrial Indemnity Company, April 1957, 5-8.
2 Denney, Reuel. *The Astonished Muse.* Chicago: University of Chicago Press, 1957.
3 Geba, Bruno Hans. *Vitality Training for Older Adults.* New York: Random House, 1974, 46-47.
4 Haun Paul. *Recreation: A Medical Viewpoint.* New York: Teachers College, Columbia University, 1965, 62.
5 Beecher, Henry K. Nonspecific Forces Surrounding Disease and the Treatment of Disease. *The Journal of the American Medical Association,* 1962, 179, 437-440.
6 Geba, Bruno Hans. The Effect of Sauna Upon Five Physiological Functions. *Dissertation Abstracts International,* 1968, 29, 4, Physiology 1484B-1485B.
7 Cannon, Walter B. Voodoo Death. *American Anthropologist,* 1942, 44:2, 169-181.
8 Richter, Curt P. On the Phenomenon of Sudden Death in Animals and Man. *Psychosomatic Medicine,* 1957, 19, 191-198.
9 Finney, J. M. T. Discussion of Shock. *Annual of Surgery,* 1934, 100, 746-747.

10 McLuhan, Marshall. *Understanding Media: The Extensions of Man.* New York: Signet Books, 1964, 23-35.

11 McLuhan, Marshall. *The Medium is the Massage.* New York: Random House, 1967.

12 McLuhan, Marshall. *Understanding Media: The Extensions of Man.* New York: Signet Books, 1964, 36-45.

13 Milan, Frederick A. The Eskimos. *National Geographic Society,* 1968, 247-248.

14 Lorenz, Konrad. *King Solomon's Ring.* New York: Thomas Y. Crowell Company, 1952, 109.

15 Uexküll, Jacob von. *Umwelt and Innenwelt der Tiere.* Berlin: Julius Springer Verlag, 1909.

16 Whorf, Benjamin Lee. *Collected Papers on Metalinguistics.* Washington: Foreign Service Institute, 1952, 21.

17 Carroll, John B. *Language, Thought and Reality.* Cambridge, Massachusetts: M.I.T. Press, 1956.

18 Rilke, Rainer Maria. Ueber Kunst. *Verse und Prosa aus dem Nachlass.* Leipzig: Deutsche Bücherei, 1929, 41-49.

19 Thoreau, Henry David. *Reflections at Walden.* Kansas City: Hallmark Cards, Inc., 1968, 33.

20 Schiller, Friedrich von. *Schillers Werke.* Salzburg, Austria: Bergland Buch Verlag, 539.

21 Egler, Frank E. Pesticides – in Our Ecosystem. *American Scientist,* 1964, 52:1, 110-136.

22 Dubos, Rene. The Gold-headed Cane in the Laboratory. *Public Health Report,* 1954, 69, 365.

23 *Diagnostic and Statistical Manual of Mental Disorders.* Washington, D.C.: American Psychiatric Association, 1980.

24 Einstein, Albert. *Briefwechsel 1916-1955.* München: Nymphenburger Verlagshandlung, 1969, 216.

25 Bacon, Roger. *Opus Majus.* Londini: Typis Gulielmi Bowyer, 1733, 446.

26 Heisenberg, Werner. Quantum Mechanics. *Physikalische Zeitschrift,* 1927, 43, 172.

27 Bohr, Niels. *Atomic Physics and Human Knowledge.* New York: Wiley, 1958, 11-23.

28 Ornstein, Donald. *Ergodic Theory, Randomness and Dynamical Systems.* New Haven: Yale University Press, 1975.

29 Hawking, Stephen W. The Quantum Mechanics of Black Holes. *Scientific American,* 1977, 40.

30 Guinness, Alec. Oscar Acceptance Speech. *Academy Awards Presentation*. Los Angeles: Harshe-Ratman and Druck, Inc., Personal Correspondence, 1980.

31 Thomas, Lewis. On Science and Uncertainty. *Discover*, 1980, 10, 58-59.

32 Bertalanffy, Ludwig von. Mind and Body Re-examined. *Journal of Humanistic Psychology*, 1966, 6, 113-138.

33 McCulloch, Warren S. *Embodiments of Mind*. Cambridge: M.I.T. Press, 1965.

PART II

1 Aristoteles. *Politics*. New York: Arno Press, 1973, II, 1271b.

2 Guinagh, Kevin. *Latin Literature in Translation*. New York: Longmans, Green and Company, 1942, 165-166.

3 Seneca, Lucius A. *Essays and Letters*. New York: W. W. Norton, 1958.

4. Bettenson, Henry. *Documents of the Christian Church*. New York: Oxford University Press, 1947, Rule XLVIII.

5 Smith, Adam. *The Wealth of Nations*. New York: Random House, 1937.

6 Leontief, Wassily W. The Distribution of Work and Income. *Scientific American*, 1982, 247:3, 188-204.

7 Hanke, F. G. *Der Endsieg des Kapitalismus*. Vienna: Verlag Orac, 1980.

8 Landers, Ann. Work Ethic a Thing of the Past? *The San Diego Evening Tribune*, May 6, 1983.

9 Russell, Bertrand. *In Praise of Idleness*. New York: Barnes and Noble, Inc., 1963, 17-18.

10 Asimov, Isaac. *I, Robot*. Garden City, New York: Doubleday, 1950.

11 Leontief, Wassily W. The Distribution of Work and Income. *Scientific American*, 1982, 247:3, 190.

12 Ginzberg, Eli. The Mechanization of Work. *Scientific American*, 1982, 247:3, 67-75.

13 Reich, Robert B. The Next American Frontier. *The Atlantic Monthly*, 1983, 4, 108.

14 Naisbitt, John. *Megatrends*. New York: Warner Books, Inc. 1982, 53.

15 Alexander, Charles P. The New Economy. *Time,* 1983, 5/30, 64.

16 Frisch, O. R. Niels Bohr. *Scientific American,* 1967, 216, 145-148.

17 Bateson, Gregory. *Steps Toward an Ecology of Mind.* San Francisco: Chandler Publishing Company, 1972, 337.

18 Allport, Gordon W. *A Handbook of Social Psychology.* Worcester, Massachusetts: Clark University Press, 1935, 798.

19 Stratton, George M. Feelings and Emotions. *The Wittenberg Symposium,* Worcester, Massachusetts: Clark University Press, 1928, 215-220.

20 Bridges, Katharine M. B. *The Social and Emotional Development of the Pre-School Child.* London: Kegan Paul, 1931, 198-211.

21 Delgado, Jose M. R. *Physical Control of the Mind.* New York: Harper & Row, 1969, 45.

22 Altman, J. Autoradiographic Studies of Postnatal Neurogenesis. *Journal of Comparative Neurology,* 1967, 128, 431-473.

23 MacLean, Paul D. The Limbic System and Its Hippocampal Formation. *Journal of Neurosurgery,* 1954, 2, 29-44.

24 Hess, Walter R. *Die Methodik der Lokalisierten Reizung.* Leipzig: Thieme, 1932.

25 Sechenov, Ivan, M. *Reflexes of the Brain.* Cambridge, Massachusetts: M.I.T. Press, 1965.

26 Piaget, Jean. *The Child's Conception of Physical Causality.* New York: Harcourt Brace & Company, 1930, 242.

27 Piaget, Jean. *The Child's Conception of the World.* London: Routledge & Kegan Paul, 1929.

28 Piaget, Jean. *The Theory of Stages in Cognitive Development.* Monterey, California: McGraw-Hill, 1969.

29 Whitman, Walt. *Leaves of Grass.* New York: Signet Classics, 1960, 73.

30 Cannon, Walter B. *Bodily Changes in Pain, Hunger, Fear and Rage.* New York: Appleton-Century-Crofts, 1929.

31 Selye, Hans. The General-Adaptation-Syndrome. *Textbook of Endocrinology.* Montreal: Montreal University, 1947.

32 Spencer, Herbert. *Essays on Education and Kindred Subjects.* London: J. M. Dent & Sons, 1910.

33 Freud, Sigmund. *Gesammelte Werke.* London: Imago Publishing Company, 1940.

34 Cousins, Norman. Anatomy of an Illness. *The New England Journal of Medicine*, 1976, 295, 26, 1458-1463.

35 Huizinga, Johan. *Homo Ludens*. Boston: Beacon Press, 1960, 4.

36 Peters, Thomas J. & Waterman, Robert H. *In Search of Excellence*. New York: Warner Books, 1984.

37 Pascale, Richard T. & Athos, Anthony G. *The Art of Japanese Management*. New York: Warner Books, 1982.

38 Geba, Bruno, Hans. *Breathe Away Your Tension*. New York: Random House, 1973, 109.

39 Carillo, Mary. In "The Zone." *World Tennis*, 1982, 29, 9, 48-51.

40 Grant, Douglas. *The Poetical Works of Charles Churchill*. Oxford: Clarendon Press, 1956, 230.

41 MacLean, Paul D. The Paranoid Streak in Man. *Beyond Reductionism*, New York: Macmillan Company, 1969, 258-278.

42 Koestler, Arthur. *The Ghost in the Machine*. New York: Macmillan Company, 1967.

43 Sperry, Roger W. Brain Mechanisms in Behavior. *Engineering and Science Monthly*, May 1957.

44 Jaynes, Julian. *The Origin of Consciousness in the Breakdown of the Bicameral Mind*. Boston: Houghton Mifflin, 1976.

45 Trotter, Robert J. The Other Hemisphere. *Science News*, 1976, 4, 218, 220, 223.

46 Shakespeare, William. Hamlet. *Shakespeare, The Complete Works*. New York: Harcourt, Brace & World, Inc., 1952.

47 Burckhardt, Jacob. *The Civilization of the Renaissance in Italy*. New York: Harper Brothers, 11, 1958, 351-352.

48 Da Vinci, Leonardo. *The Notebooks of Leonardo Da Vinci*. New York: Reynal & Hitchcock, 1938, 2, 509.

49 Lorenz, Konrad. *Das Sogenannte Böse*. Wien: Borotha-Schoeler Verlag, 1963.

50 Calvin. *Institutes of the Christian Religion*. Philadelphia: The Westminster Press, 1967, 253.

51 Gay, Peter. *The Science of Freedom*. New York: Alfred A. Knopf, 1970.

52 Szasz, Thomas, S. *The Myth of Mental Illness*. New York: Harper & Row, 1954.

53 Szasz, Thomas, S. *Law, Liberty, and Psychiatry*. New York: Collier Books, 1968, 11-17.

54 Maslow, Abraham H. *Motivation and Personality*. New York: Harper & Row, 1954.

55 Janov, Arthur. *The Primal Scream.* New York: Dell Publishing Company, 1970.

56 Bertalanffy, Ludwig von. *Biophysik des Fliessgleichgewichtes.* Braunschweig, 1953.

57 Bertalanffy, Ludwig von. *Robots, Men and Minds.* New York: Braziller, 1967, 70.

58 Rapoport, Anatol. Modern Systems Theory. *General Systems Yearbook,* 1970, 15, 15-25.

59 Maslow, Abraham H. *The Psychology of Science.* Chicago: Henry Regency, 1966.

60 Laszlo, E. *An Introduction to Systems Philosophy.* New York: Harper & Row, 1972, 4.

61 Shubik, Martin. The Uses of Game Theory. *Contemporary Political Analysis.* New York: Free Press, 1967, 240.

62 Spiro, Herbert J. An Evaluation of Systems Theory. *Contemporary Political Analysis.* New York: Free Press, 1967, 165.

63 Tinbergen, N. *Social Behavior in Animals.* London: Methuen, 1953, 130.

64 Churchill, Winston. *Onwards to Victory.* Boston: Little Brown, 1944, 316-317.

65 Camus, Albert. *Resistance, Rebellion, and Death.* New York: Alfred A. Knopf, 1961, 206.

66 Nietzsche, Friedrich. *Nietzsches Werke.* Salzburg, Austria: Bergland Buch Verlag, 889-937.

67 Dubos, Rene. *The Wooing of the Earth.* New York: Charles Scribner's Sons, 1980, 160-161.

68 Bohm, David. *Wholeness and the Implicate Order.* London: Routledge & Kegan Paul, 1980.

69 Sivard, Ruth Leger. *World Military and Social Expenditures.* Leesburg, Virginia: World Priorities, 1982, 11.

70 Wells, H. G. *The Common Sense of World Peace.* London: L. & Virginia Woolf, 1929.

71 Plato. *The Apology of Socrates.* Cambridge: Cambridge University Press, 1976, 38a.

72 Dubos, Rene. *Beast or Angel?* New York: Charles Scribner's Sons, 1974, 204.

 **LEISURE**
SCIENCE
SYSTEMS INTERNATIONAL

P.O. Box 3832 • La Mesa, CA 92041 • USA • 619/265-4451
CONSULTATION • EDUCATION • PUBLICATION

ORDER BLANK

BEING AT LEISURE–PLAYING AT LIFE
A Guide to Health and Joyful Living

by BRUNO HANS GEBA

Quantity	Description	Price	Tax*	Total
	Paperback	$14.95	$ .90	
	Hardcover	$19.95	$1.20	
		Shipping**		
			TOTAL	

*Sales Tax for California Residents only.
**Shipping for first Paperback $1.15
　　　　　for first Hardcover $1.35
　　　　　each additional book   .25¢

Request discount schedule when ordering ten or more books.

Check_____　　　Money Order_____

Payable to:　L.S.S.I.
　　　　　　P.O. Box 3832
　　　　　　La Mesa, CA 92041

Your Address:

Name_____

Street_____

City _____

State_____　Zip_____